D1303801

Chocolate Heaven

Chocolate Heaven

The Ultimate Indulgence

Elizabeth Wolf Cohen
and
Valerie Barrett

JG PRESS

A QUINTET BOOK

Published in the USA 1995 by JG Press.
Distributed by World Publications, Inc.

The JG Press imprint is a trademark of
JG Press, Inc.
455 Somerset Avenue, North Dighton, MA 02764

This edition produced for sale in the USA, its territories and
dependencies only.

Copyright © 1995 Quintet Publishing Limited.
All rights reserved. No part of this publication may be reproduced, stored
in a retrieval system or transmitted in any form or by any means,
electronic, mechanical, photocopying, recording or otherwise, without the
permission of the copyright holder.

ISBN 1-57215-061-0

The material in this book previously appeared in *The Chocolate Cookbook*
by Elizabeth Wolf Cohen, and *The Chocolate Book* by Valerie Barrett.

This book was designed and produced by
Quintet Publishing Limited
6 Blundell Street
London N7 9BH

Creative Director: Richard Dewing
Designer: Isobel Gillan
Editor: Diana Vowles

Typeset in Great Britain by
Central Southern Typesetters, Eastbourne
Manufactured by Eray Scan Pte Ltd, Singapore
Printed by Star Standard Industries (Pte) Ltd, Singapore

CONTENTS

Introduction

The History of Chocolate

Smooth, rich chocolate in its many present day variations has its origins in a simple brown bean. The cocoa bean grows on the cocoa tree and it is believed that the trees originally grew wild in the Amazon. It is probable that when the Mayans migrated to the Yucatan in about AD 600 they established the first cocoa plantations. The Aztecs also used the beans and would have carried them on their travels in Central America.

The beans fulfilled two purposes. They were used as currency: it is said that 10 beans would buy a rabbit and 100 would buy a slave! The other use to which the cocoa bean was put was as the basis of a bitter, foamy drink which had religious and ceremonial significance. This drink, called *chocolatl* (bitter water) was made by mixing roasted ground beans with water or wine which was then beaten until frothy.

Christopher Columbus has been credited with discovering America and as being the first European to see cocoa beans and probably to taste the drink. He returned to the Spanish court with some beans, but they aroused little interest, perhaps because Columbus himself was more interested in his search for new routes to the East. Nothing more happened on the chocolate front for about 17 years until the Spanish explorer Cortez conquered Mexico in 1519. Cortez and his Spanish Conquistadors were invited to the magnificent Aztec court of the Emperor Montezuma. Although Cortez disliked the drink, he was impressed by the way it was served in ornate golden goblets and with the quantity drunk by the Emperor and his intimates. He was also quick to recognize the value of the bean as a currency. Cortez therefore established his own cocoa plantation under the Spanish flag. When the Spanish left Mexico,

they took some beans with them and planted them in various places as they traveled. Once home, Cortez introduced the chocolate drink to the Spanish court. As the drink was pungent and bitter the Spaniards added sugar and vanilla to it. These additions made the drink much more palatable and it quickly became very popular at court and in high society. The Spanish began to plant more and more cocoa overseas, but they kept the secret of its preparation for almost 100 years.

In 1606 an Italian called Antonio Carlotti took the recipe to Italy. From then on the drink spread throughout Europe. When Anne of Austria married Louis XIII of France she brought her own chocolate with her and when the Spanish princess Marie Thérèse married Louis XIV, chocolate was drunk at court, a royal chocolate maker was appointed and chocolate drinking became the rage. Coffee houses, which were already established meeting-places in England, were now joined by chocolate houses. These places were the precursors of our present-day cafés and bars and they were frequented by politicians, writers and socialites.

The first chocolate factory in America was set up in New England in 1765. Similar factories were also springing up in Europe; Dr Joseph Fry was the first Englishman to manufacture chocolate in a big way. The real breakthrough came in 1828 when a Dutchman called C Van Houten patented a process whereby cocoa powder and extract cocoa butter could be obtained from the cocoa mass. Up until this time the whole bean had been ground and used, resulting in a "fatty" drink. Van Houten's cocoa press squeezed out some of the cocoa butter, leaving behind what we now know as cocoa powder. Twenty years later Joseph Fry discovered how to combine the extracted cocoa butter with the chocolate liquor and sugar to make "eating" chocolate, and in Switzerland, in 1875, Daniel Peter added condensed milk to chocolate and marketed the first solid milk chocolate bar.

LEFT *Classic Devil's Food Cake*

A few years later Rodolphe Lindt invented a way of refining chocolate. As long as chocolate was made into a drink it didn't matter if it had lumps and gritty bits as these tended to dissolve or sink with the addition of liquid. However, a solid chocolate bar was a different matter. Lindt's process, which became known as "conching," consisted of putting the chocolate in heated drums for about 72 hours and rubbing it between rollers or discs. This process gives a silky smoothness to chocolate, allowing it to be poured into different molds rather than just pressed into "cakes."

Since then, the technological changes in the manufacture of chocolate and chocolate products have come fast and furious. From being a luxury that only the rich could afford, chocolate is now an everyday commodity that we take for granted.

How Chocolate is Grown and Made

The cocoa bean which gives us both cocoa and chocolate is grown in pods on the cocoa tree (*Theobroma cacao*). The first cocoa trees probably originated in the Amazon forest more than 4000 years ago. Because the tree requires a tropical climate, it is cultivated only in West Africa, northern and central South America, the Caribbean and some parts of Asia between the tropics of Cancer and Capricorn.

The cocoa tree is extremely sensitive and so the young seeds are grown in special nurseries. After a few months they are transplanted to the cocoa plantation. They need protection from wind and excessive sunlight. This is often provided by banana, coconut or lemon trees, known as "cocoa mothers," which are planted nearby.

By the time the tree is four or five years old it has dark glossy leaves and ripe fruit in the form of pods growing on both the branches and the trunk. An evergreen, the tree is not dissimilar in size and shape to an English apple tree. The pods are about 3–4 inches wide and 6–10 inches long and are elongated ovals in shape. When young they are a green or red color and as they ripen the outer shells become hard and turn golden or bright red. Inside the pod are between 20 and 50 plump almond-shaped seeds surrounded by a whitish pulp. These seeds are the precious cocoa beans.

On most plantations there are two harvest seasons, each lasting about three months. The pods are cut down from the trees with large steel knives or machetes, collected in baskets and taken to be opened. Once they are split apart the beans and pulp are scooped out. At first the beans are creamy in color, but as they are exposed to the air they change to purple. The pulp and the seeds are put into large heaps either on the ground or in boxes or baskets, covered with leaves and left to ferment. The white pulp ferments and produces alcohol and other by-products. The temperature rises and kills off the germ in the cocoa beans so that they cannot sprout, and starts a chain of chemical reactions that remove the bitterness and develop the characteristic chocolate flavor. At the end of fermentation, which can take from two to six days, the beans have turned brown and have become separated from the pulp. They are still wet and have to be spread out in the sun or dried with hot-air blowers to prevent them from rotting. At this stage, checks are made for defects, such as mold or insect damage. The sun gives the beans an even deeper color and a more aromatic flavor.

The beans are then put into sacks and sent all over the world to various processing plants.

On arrival at the factory, the beans are cleaned and sorted. They are then roasted in a similar way to coffee beans. During roasting the beans become darker brown, the shell becomes brittle and the beans take on their full

"chocolate" aroma. The roasted beans are now put into a machine which cracks them open and an artificial wind or winnower blows away the brittle shell, leaving behind the cocoa "nibs."

The nibs are ground between rollers to produce a thick dark paste or "chocolate liquor" called the "mass." It hardens on cooling and is sometimes formed into bars at this stage to be sold as unsweetened baking chocolate. This mass or chocolate liquor is the basis of all chocolate and cocoa products.

To make cocoa powder, the chocolate liquor is poured into a press. A good percentage of the cocoa butter (a fatty substance which is found in the bean) is pressed out. This leaves a solid, dry cake which is then crushed, ground and sifted. The end result of this process is cocoa powder. Cocoa powder is sold just as it is, or it can be mixed with a variety of ingredients such as sugar, starches and milk to produce drinking chocolate or chocolate malted drinks.

Whereas cocoa is made by extracting cocoa butter from the chocolate liquor, chocolate is made by adding extra cocoa butter to it. Adding sugar produces "semisweet" chocolate; adding milk and sugar produces "milk" chocolate. "White" chocolate is made from cocoa butter only, with the addition of sugar and milk.

When the various ingredients are added to the liquor they are blended in a mixing machine. At this point the mixture is still gritty, so it goes through a series of heavy rollers called a refiner. After this the chocolate is smooth, but to make it really silky on the tongue, it goes through a final stirring treatment known as "conching." This takes place in large drums or conches (from the Spanish *concha*, meaning shell) in which the chocolate is heated and kneaded with rollers. After conching, the liquid chocolate is tempered or cooled so that the fat begins to harden and the chocolate can then be molded. The filled molds are cooled, the chocolate removed, wrapped and sent to the stores. So ends the journey from cocoa bean to chocolate bar.

TYPES OF CHOCOLATE

Unsweetened Chocolate

Unsweetened chocolate is also known as "cooking," "baking" or "baker's chocolate." The nearest substitute, if it is unobtainable, is always to use 3 tablespoons cocoa and 1 tablespoon fat to replace 1 oz unsweetened chocolate. The flavor of unsweetened chocolate is bitter, intense and full-bodied, as it has no sugar or flavorings added.

Bitter Chocolate

Bitter chocolate is available in some delicatessens (Van Houten, Lindt, and Suchard are popular brands) and it can be used instead of semisweet chocolate for a strong flavor.

Couverture Chocolate

Couverture chocolate contains a high proportion of cocoa butter, which makes it very smooth and glossy. As it has a very brittle texture it needs "tempering" before use (see page 13). This type of chocolate is used normally by professionals. However, it is excellent for coating and molding and well worth buying if you do a lot of chocolate cooking.

Milk Chocolate

Milk chocolate has a much milder flavor than semisweet as some of the chocolate has been replaced by milk solids. It is best to use this chocolate only in recipes that specifically call for it.

Chocolate Cake Covering or "Coating" Chocolate

This should not be confused with semisweet or milk chocolate as it has a certain amount of the cocoa butter replaced by coconut, palm kernel oil or some other vegetable fat. It is much cheaper than semisweet chocolate and, because it is very easily melted, it is easier to handle. It is good for decorative chocolate recipes and for covering or coating cakes, as it does not streak. The only disadvantage is that the flavor is not as strong as that of semisweet chocolate.

Dipping Chocolate

This chocolate makes a good alternative to couverture chocolate. It contains a high proportion of vegetable fat and is good for dipping and molding.

Semisweet Chocolate

Semisweet eating chocolate has a good strong flavor and is the most suited for use in cake, dessert and candy recipes. Semisweet chocolate is made with chocolate liquor, cocoa butter, vegetable fats, sugar and flavorings.

Cocoa Powder

This is chocolate from which the cocoa butter has been removed, before being ground into a powder. Dutch cocoa powder, if available, is darker and slightly less bitter than most as it has been treated with an alkali. Cocoa can be used dry and sifted with other dry ingredients such as flour or powdered sugar before being incorporated into a recipe. In some recipes it is better to mix the cocoa to a paste with hot water, thus breaking down the starch cells before cooking.

Drinking Chocolate

Drinking chocolate is cocoa with a high proportion of sugar. It has a mild, very sweet flavor. Apart from its obvious use in drinks it can be useful as a coating on such things as truffles.

White Chocolate

This is not really a chocolate at all. It is made from milk, sugar and cocoa butter or another vegetable fat. It is not normally used for cooking, but if you do wish to experiment take great care when melting it as it can very easily become tight and grainy.

COOKING WITH CHOCOLATE

Cooking with chocolate as the main ingredient can be quite spectacular, especially when other good-quality ingredients are used. To prevent disappointment, you must remember to treat chocolate with TLC: tender loving care.

Melting Chocolate

There are several different ways to melt chocolate, but if you wish to avoid ending up with a solid mass there are a few rules which must be observed. Any equipment used must be perfectly dry because any stray drops of water will cause the chocolate to thicken and stiffen. For the same reason, never cover chocolate when it is being, or has already been, melted. If you do end up with a solid mass, try stirring in a little vegetable oil and mix very well. Butter or margarine will not do as they contain some water. The second thing to remember is *never* to rush the melting process. A watched pot never boils and the temptation is to turn up the heat and speed up the process. Unfortunately this will ruin the flavor and texture of the chocolate. It is best to grate or chop the chocolate before melting for a smooth result.

Direct Heat Method

This method is only used when the chocolate is combined with butter, sugar or milk, or similar ingredients, as when making some candies and sauces. The mixture should always be stirred over a very gentle heat. As soon as the mixture has melted it should be removed from the heat to prevent the chocolate over-cooking and becoming "grainy."

Double Boiler Method

This is probably one of the best and easiest methods of melting chocolate. If you do not possess a double boiler, one can easily be made by placing a heatproof bowl over a saucepan. The bowl should fit securely on the pan so that neither steam nor water can escape. The water in the saucepan should never touch the bottom of the bowl. Place the chocolate in the bowl. Allow the water in the saucepan to come to the boil and place the bowl on top. Turn off the heat under the saucepan and leave to stand for a while until the chocolate is melted.

Oven Method

Chocolate may be melted in an ovenproof bowl in a very low oven (225°F). If the oven has been in use for another purpose and has been turned off, it makes sense to use the lingering heat to melt the chocolate. When the chocolate has almost melted it should be removed and stirred until smooth.

Microwave Oven Method

Microwave ovens are very handy for melting chocolate, especially small quantities, quickly and safely. The chocolate should be broken into small pieces and put into a glass bowl. Microwave, uncovered, until almost melted. The manufacturer's instructions should be followed as the timing and power setting will vary according to the machine.

On average, 3 oz chocolate will melt in 1–1½ minutes. It is important to stir the chocolate just before the end of the cooking time to see if the chocolate has melted and thus prevent overcooking.

Double boiler method

How to "Temper" Couverture Chocolate

Generally speaking couverture chocolate is only used by professionals and so is not readily available in stores. However, if you wish to do a lot of chocolate cookery, especially dipping or using molds, it is worth getting hold of some. Because couverture has a high cocoa butter content it flows and coats excellently. Couverture chocolate must be tempered before using. To do this you will need a thermometer. Break up the chocolate and melt by the double boiler method. Heat the chocolate to a temperature of 100–115°F. Stir well during this heating process. The chocolate then has to be cooled. To do this, remove the bowl to a pan of cold water and cool to 80–82°F, stirring thoroughly. Return the chocolate to the double boiler and reheat to 88–90°F. Stir all the time and do not exceed this final temperature. The chocolate is now ready to be used. If there is chocolate left over at the end, it can be reheated without further tempering.

Chocolate for Dipping

Truffles, caramels and other candies, as well as fresh or dried fruit pieces, can all be dipped in chocolate. Use either tempered couverture or dipping or semisweet chocolate. Heat in a double boiler. The ideal temperature for dipping is 92–110°F. The temperature should never exceed 120°F. The chocolate should be in a bowl deep enough for the confection to be totally covered. Using a special dipping fork, fondue fork, or thin skewer, lower the confection into the chocolate. Turn it over and then lift out the chocolate, tapping the fork on the edge of the bowl to shake off the excess chocolate. Place the chocolate on a baking sheet lined with waxed paper. The dipping fork can be used to decorate the top of the chocolates before they set. Lay the fork on the surface of the chocolate and lift it gently to create ridges.

Using Molds

Special molds can be bought to make eggs, animals (such as rabbits or mice), boxes and so on. They are available in metal or plastic. The plastic ones are cheaper and easier to use in that you can see when the chocolate has shrunk from the sides. The mold must be extremely clean so the chocolate does not stick and has a shiny surface. Wash, rinse, and dry the mold thoroughly. Polish well with a soft cloth or paper towel, as an abrasive material may scratch and cause the chocolate to stick.

It is best to use a chocolate that will set hard, so always choose dipping, couverture, or good-quality semisweet eating chocolate. Melt the chocolate over hot

water. The amount will vary according to the size of the mold. Very small molds will only need one layer, but larger ones will need two, three or four layers. The larger the mold, the thicker the chocolate layer needs to be. Pour the melted chocolate into the mold. Tilt and rotate the mold so that the chocolate coats it evenly. Tip out any excess chocolate. Turn the mold upside down onto a baking sheet lined with waxed paper. Put it in a cool place (*not* the refrigerator) until the first layer is just firm to the touch. Repeat as above for subsequent layers. Leave the chocolate to set hard. The chocolate should have shrunk away from the mold when it is ready.

Very carefully scrape away any chocolate that has gone over the edge of the mold. Gently pull or shake the shape out of the mold. Be careful not to mark the outside with fingerprints! Place the shapes on waxed paper. To stick two halves together, as for an Easter egg, brush a little melted chocolate round the rim and press the two halves together. Melted chocolate or frosting can be used to pipe over any joins on the outside.

STORING CHOCOLATE

Chocolate should be kept in a cool dry place. Contrary to popular belief the refrigerator is not the best place to store chocolate other than for short periods during hot weather. When refrigerated, chocolate will absorb odors very easily and also may collect a film of moisture on the surface, so wrap the chocolate in foil then in a plastic bag if you wish to refrigerate it. Let the chocolate stand at room temperature before unwrapping and using, as this should prevent moisture condensing on the surface.

If chocolate is stored in very warm conditions the cocoa butter or sugar crystals in it may rise to the surface, giving a grayish white "bloom." This is completely harmless and although it detracts from the appearance it does not affect the flavor of the chocolate. The bloom will disappear on melting so the chocolate is quite suitable for cooking.

If you wish to keep chocolate for a longer time in hot conditions, then it is best to freeze it. Again, make sure it is tightly wrapped. Remove it from the freezer the night before you need it, and allow it to thaw completely before unwrapping it. The freezer is an especially good place to store chocolate decorations such as squares, leaves, and so on. These can then be used any time to garnish cakes and desserts and only need a few hours to thaw.

If kept in the correct conditions, semisweet chocolate should keep for one year and milk chocolate for about six months.

USEFUL EQUIPMENT FOR CHOCOLATE COOKING

Grater

For grating chocolate, you will need a stainless steel box or conical-shaped grater with varied cutting edges.

Potato Peeler

A potato peeler is used for making chocolate curls. The type that has a fixed blade is best.

Skewers or Toothpicks

These are useful for dipping or the lifting and placing of delicate chocolate decorations.

Dipping Forks

These are usually about 8 inches long, made of stainless steel with wooden handles. They are available in a variety of shapes, from two, three, and four prongs to round, spiral, or triangular shapes. As well as dipping, the forks can be used for marking designs on top of the chocolates.

Double Boiler

Best made of stainless steel or enameled steel, this consists of two pans, one made to rest on top and slightly inside the other. Hot water is placed in the bottom pan and the chocolate is melted in the top.

Sugar Boiling Thermometer

Made of brass, the thermometer should be well graduated up to 400°F. It is essential for certain candy recipes and also for tempering couverture chocolate.

Cutters

You will need a selection of various sizes and shapes in steel or plastic. There are very many available now and some make lovely chocolate decorations.

Candy and Cupcake Papers

These are available in different sizes and qualities. If they are to be used for making chocolate cups, choose foil if you can, or else a sturdy paper type.

Piping Bags and Nozzles

For piping chocolate, medium or small bags are best. In fact, for piping small amounts of chocolate in decorative work it is better to make bags from waxed paper. Star, rope and plain nozzles are the most useful to have.

Marble Slab

Not essential, but useful to have for chocolate work as it keeps everything cool.

Chocolate Draining Tray

This is similar to a cooling rack, but with a smaller wire mesh.

Waxed Paper

Waxed paper is ideal for lining pans or baking sheets when working with chocolate.

Molds

Several different types are available. One type is made of tin, with two halves which clip together when setting. This type makes a solid mold. Other types come in one "half" of a shape and are used to make hollow molds.

Icing Comb

Made of plastic or metal, this is useful for making ridged designs on chocolate, such as when making florentines.

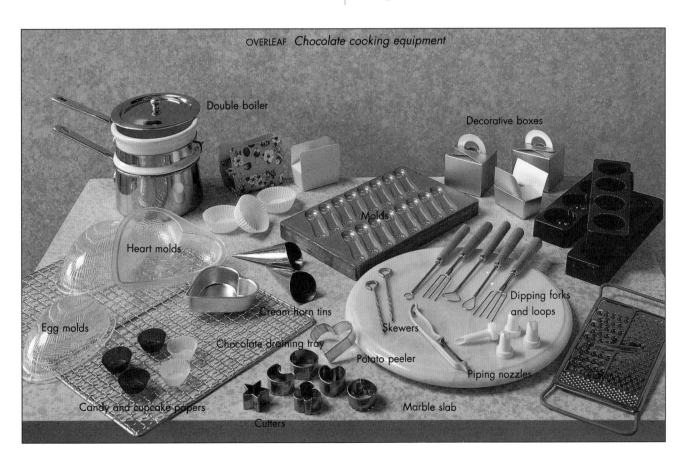

OVERLEAF *Chocolate cooking equipment*

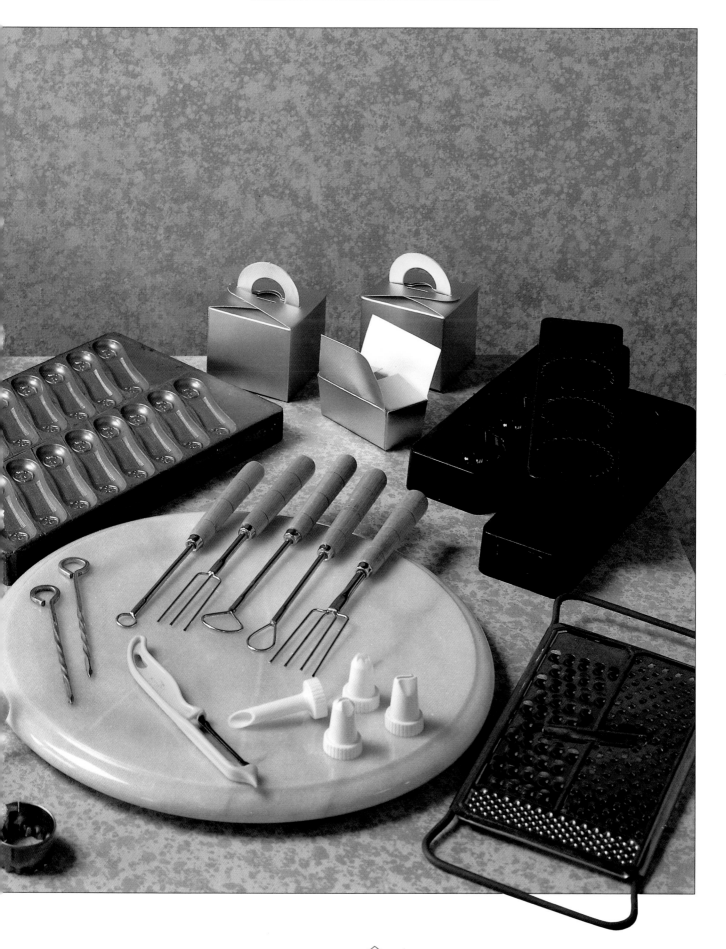

MAKING CHOCOLATE DECORATIONS

Grated Chocolate

Chill the chocolate and then rub it across a hand grater. Use either the fine grater or the large grater, depending on the dish you wish to garnish. To prevent clogging, brush the grater every now and then with a dry pastry brush.

Chocolate Scrolls

Melt some baking or semisweet chocolate and spread out on a cool work surface to a thickness of about ⅛ inch. Cool until set, but not hard. Hold a long firm knife at an angle of 45° under the chocolate and push it away from you, scraping off long curls.

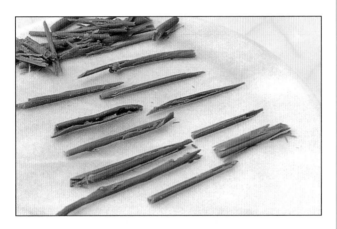

Chocolate Curls

Use chocolate at room temperature (if the chocolate is too cold the curls will break, and if it is too hot they will not curl at all). It is best to use a very thick bar of chocolate. Holding the bar over a plate, draw the blade of a vegetable peeler along the edge and allow the curls to fall onto the plate. Use a toothpick to lift the curls on to the dish to be decorated.

Chocolate Caraque

Melt and spread some chocolate as for chocolate scrolls. Place a sharp-pointed, long-bladed knife on the surface of the chocolate. Keep the tip of the knife securely in one place. Holding the knife at a slight angle, scrape in a quarter circle movement to produce long, thin, slightly cone-shaped curls.

Chopped Chocolate

Use chocolate at room temperature. Break into small pieces and place on a chopping board. Using a sharp chopping knife, chop into the size required. Chocolate may also be chopped quite successfully in a food processor.

Chocolate Squares, Triangles, Rectangles and Wedges

Melt baking or semisweet chocolate and spread evenly on waxed paper. Leave to set. Using a ruler, mark into squares or rectangles. Cut with a sharp knife. The squares may be cut diagonally to form triangles and the rectangles cut diagonally to form wedges.

Chocolate Cups

Use two thicknesses of cupcake papers or candy papers. (If you can obtain foil cases a single layer only is necessary.) Melt the chocolate and brush on the bottom and up the sides of the cases. Repeat this process until a thick layer is obtained. Carefully turn upside down onto waxed paper. Chill until hard. Peel the paper away from the chocolate and fill as desired.

Chocolate Cut-outs

Melt baking or semisweet chocolate and spread evenly on waxed paper. Leave to set. Using cookie cutters, stamp out shapes, such as hearts, crescents, stars, animals, letters, and so on.

Piped Designs

Trace the chosen design lightly on a piece of waxed paper. Melt the chocolate and pour into a piping bag, fitted with a small plain nozzle. Follow the outline of the design first. Either fill in the centers with solid chocolate or pipe a "lace" infill. Ideas for piped designs:

Holly leaves: Pipe outlines and then fill in centres.

Simple flower shapes: Pipe any flower shape that appeals to you, such as a daisy.

Chocolate filigree fans: Outline a fan shape and fill in with "lace" work.

Butterflies: Cut waxed paper into small squares. Pipe chocolate onto the paper in a butterfly outline. Fill in the wings with additional lines. Leave until beginning to set. Transfer to an upturned egg carton, placing the butterfly between the cups so it is bent in the centre in the shape of a butterfly. Chill. Carefully remove the paper and position on the chosen dish.

Chocolate Leaves

Select non-toxic fresh leaves with clearly defined veins, such as rose, bay, ivy, strawberry, or mint. Wash the leaves and pat dry. Melt some chocolate on a heatproof plate over a pan of hot water. Holding the leaf by the stem, carefully dip the veined side only into the chocolate. Alternatively, brush the chocolate on the leaf with a small paintbrush. Wipe off any chocolate that may have run onto the front of the leaf. Place on waxed paper to set. When the chocolate is completely hard, carefully pull off the leaf by the stem.

Chocolate Horns

To make chocolate horns you will need cream horn tins. Make sure the tins are clean and dry, and polish the inside well with paper towels. Pour a little melted chocolate into the tin, and tilt and turn it until evenly coated. Repeat this process until a thick layer of chocolate is coating the inside of the mold. Leave to set. The chocolate should shrink slightly away from the mold when hard and can be carefully eased out with the point of a knife.

Chocolate-coated ice cream cones can be made in a similar manner. After coating the insides of the ice cream cones with chocolate they can be placed in the freezer for about 10 minutes to harden. They should then be filled with scoops of ice cream and eaten immediately.

COOKIES

Chocolate Crackle Tops

MAKES ABOUT 38

7 oz semisweet chocolate, chopped
⅓ cup + 1 tbsp unsalted butter
⅔ cup fine granulated sugar
3 eggs
1 tbsp vanilla extract
¼ cup flour
2 tbsp cocoa powder
½ tsp baking powder
¼ tsp salt
1¼–1½ cups powdered sugar for coating

SWEET SUCCESS

These cookies are best eaten as fresh as possible, but they will last for several days in an airtight container.

◆ In a saucepan over low heat, melt the chocolate and butter, stirring frequently until smooth. Remove from the heat. Stir in the sugar and continue stirring for 2-3 minutes, until the sugar dissolves. Add the eggs, 1 at a time, beating well after each addition, then stir in the vanilla extract.

◆ Into a bowl, sift together the flour, cocoa powder, baking powder and salt. Gradually stir into the chocolate mixture in batches just until blended. Cover the dough and refrigerate for 2-3 hours or overnight, until the dough is cold and holds its shape.

◆ Preheat the oven to 325°F. Grease 2 or more large baking sheets. Place powdered sugar in a small, deep bowl. Using a small ice cream scoop, about 1 inch in diameter, or a teaspoon, scoop the cold dough into small balls.

◆ Between the palms of your hands, roll the dough into 1½ inch balls. Drop the balls, 1 at a time, into powdered sugar and roll until heavily coated. Remove each ball with a slotted spoon and tap against the side of the bowl to remove excess sugar. Place on baking sheets 1½ inches apart. Use more powdered sugar as necessary; you may need to cook in batches.

◆ Bake the cookies for 10-12 minutes, or until top of cookie feels slightly firm when touched with fingertip; do not overbake or cookies will be dry. Transfer the baking sheets to a wire rack for 2-3 minutes, just until the cookies are set. With a metal spatula, transfer the cookies to a wire rack to cool completely.

Chocolate Chunk Chocolate Drops

MAKES ABOUT 18

6 oz semisweet chocolate, chopped
½ cup unsalted butter, cut
into pieces
2 eggs
½ cup sugar
¼ cup brown sugar
3 tbsp flour
2 tbsp cocoa powder
1 tsp baking powder
2 tsp vanilla extract
¼ tsp salt
¼ cup pecans, toasted and chopped
6 oz semisweet chocolate chips
4 oz good-quality white chocolate,
chopped into ¼ inch pieces
4 oz good-quality milk chocolate,
chopped into ¼ inch pieces

◆ Preheat the oven to 325°F. Grease 2 large baking sheets. In a medium saucepan over low heat, melt the chocolate and butter, stirring frequently until smooth. Remove from the heat to cool slightly.

◆ With an electric mixer, beat the eggs and sugars until thick and pale, 2-3 minutes. Gradually pour in the melted chocolate, beating until well blended. Beat in the flour, cocoa powder, baking powder, vanilla extract, and salt just until blended. Stir in the nuts, chocolate chips and chocolate pieces.

◆ Drop heaping tablespoonfuls of dough on the baking sheets at least 4 inches apart, flattening the dough slightly, trying to keep about a 3 inch circle; you will only get 4-6 cookies on each sheet. Bake for 10-12 minutes, until the tops are cracked and shiny; do not overbake or they will break when removed from the baking sheet.

◆ Remove the baking sheets to a wire rack to cool until the cookies are firm, but not too crisp. Before they become too crisp, transfer each cookie to a wire rack to cool completely. Continue to bake in batches. Store the cookies in an airtight container.

SWEET SUCCESS

If you need to use the same baking sheets to bake in batches, cool by running the back of the baking sheet under cold water and wiping the surface with a paper towel before regreasing.

Chocolate Amaretti Cookies

MAKES ABOUT 24

a scant 1 cup blanched whole almonds
½ cup fine granulated sugar
1 tbsp cocoa powder
2 tbsp powdered sugar
2 egg whites
pinch of cream of tartar
1 tsp almond extract
powdered sugar for dusting

◆ Preheat the oven to 350°F. Place the almonds on a small baking sheet and bake for 10-12 minutes, stirring occasionally, until golden brown. Remove from the oven and cool to room temperature; reduce the oven temperature to 325°F. Line a large baking sheet with waxed paper or foil.

◆ In a food processor fitted with the metal blade, process the almonds with ¼ cup sugar until the almonds are finely ground, but not oily. Transfer to a bowl and sift in the cocoa powder and powdered sugar; stir to blend. Set aside.

◆ With an electric mixer, beat the egg whites and cream of tartar until soft peaks form. Sprinkle in the remaining sugar, 1 tbsp at a time, beating well after each addition, until the whites are glossy and stiff. Beat in the almond extract.

◆ Sprinkle the almond sugar mixture over and gently fold into the beaten whites just until blended. Spoon the mixture into a large piping bag fitted with a plain ½ inch nozzle. Pipe 1½ inch circles about 1 inch apart onto the prepared baking sheet.

◆ Bake for 12-15 minutes, or until the cookies appear crisp. Transfer the baking sheets to a wire rack to cool for 10 minutes. With a metal spatula, transfer the cookies to a wire rack to cool completely. When cool, dust with powdered sugar and store in an airtight container.

VARIATION

As an alternative decoration, lightly press a few coffee-sugar crystals onto top of each cookie before baking.

Chocolate Chip Cookies

MAKES ABOUT 30

½ cup self-rising flour
2 tbsp unsweetened cocoa powder
½ tsp baking powder
½ cup butter or margarine
½ cup brown sugar
¼ cup sugar
2 eggs
½ tsp vanilla extract
¼ cup chocolate chips
½ cup chopped walnuts

◆ Preheat the oven to 375°F. Sift together the flour, cocoa and baking powder.
◆ Beat together the butter or margarine and sugars until light and fluffy.
◆ Beat in the eggs one at a time. Add the vanilla extract.
◆ Add the dry ingredients and beat until well combined.
◆ Stir in the chocolate chips and nuts.
◆ Drop the dough in heaping teaspoonfuls onto a baking sheet. Bake in the oven for about 10 minutes.
◆ Cool for a minute then remove from the baking sheet and cool on a wire rack.

Bittersweet Fudge Cookies

MAKES ABOUT 36

6 oz bitter chocolate, chopped
½ cup unsalted butter, at room temperature
½ cup sugar
2 eggs
1 tsp vanilla extract
¼ cup all-purpose flour
½ tsp salt
¼ cup pecans, chopped and toasted
3 oz good-quality white chocolate, chopped into ¼ inch pieces
melted chocolate, to decorate

◆ In the top of a double boiler over low heat, melt the chocolate, stirring frequently until smooth. Remove from the heat.

◆ With an electric mixer, cream the butter, sugar, eggs, and vanilla extract until creamy and smooth, 2-3 minutes, scraping the bowl occasionally. Slowly beat in the cooled chocolate until well blended.
◆ Gradually stir in the flour and salt, stirring just until blended. Stir in the pecans and chopped white chocolate. Cover the bowl with plastic wrap and refrigerate for 1 hour or until firm.
◆ Meanwhile, preheat the oven to 375°F. Lightly grease 2 large baking sheets. Drop rounded teaspoonfuls of dough at least 2 inches apart onto the prepared baking sheets, flattening slightly. You may need to cook them in 2 batches.
◆ Bake for 8-10 minutes, or just until the surface feels slightly firm when touched with a fingertip. Remove the baking sheets to wire racks to cool for 5-7 minutes. With a metal spatula, remove the cookies to a wire rack to cool completely. Repeat with the remaining dough. When cool, drizzle chocolate over them using a spoon. Store in airtight containers.

Chocolate Pinwheels

MAKES ABOUT 40

¼ cup butter or margarine
¼ cup sugar
1 large egg, beaten
1 tsp vanilla extract
1½ cups self-rising flour
3 tbsp unsweetened cocoa powder
a little beaten egg white

◆ Put the butter or margarine and sugar into a bowl and cream together until light and fluffy.
◆ Beat in the egg and vanilla extract.
◆ Work the flour into the creamed mixture.
◆ Divide the mixture in half and knead the cocoa into one half. Shape into 2 smooth balls. Wrap in plastic wrap and chill.

◆ To make pinwheel cookies, roll out the plain and chocolate doughs separately into equal rectangles. Brush the plain dough with egg white and place the chocolate mixture on top. Brush the chocolate mixture with egg white.
◆ Roll up like a jelly roll. Wrap in foil and chill.
◆ Cut into ¼ inch thick slices. Place on a baking sheet and bake in a preheated oven at 375°F for about 8 minutes.

VARIATIONS

◆ To make checkerboard cookies, reserve about a quarter of the plain dough.
◆ Shape the remaining plain and chocolate doughs each into 2 long thin rolls. Brush with egg white.
◆ Put a chocolate roll next to a plain roll. Place the other 2 rolls on top, reversing the colors. Press lightly together.

◆ Roll out the reserved plain dough to a large rectangle. Brush with egg white and roll it around the 4 thin rolls. Chill, slice and cook as in recipe above.
◆ To make owl cookies, roll out the plain mixture to a rectangle.
◆ Form the chocolate mixture into a roll. Brush with egg white and roll up in the plain mixture.
◆ Wrap and chill.
◆ Cut into ¼ inch slices.
◆ To form the owl's head, put 2 circles side by side. Brush the join with egg white and press lightly together.
◆ Pinch the top corners of each head to form ears.
◆ Place almond halves in the center of each head for the beak. Put 2 chocolate dots for the eyes.
◆ Cook as in the main recipe.

Chocolate-Mint Sandwich Cookies

MAKES ABOUT 20

½ cup unsalted butter, softened
¼ cup sugar
1 egg
½ cup butter or margarine
1 tsp peppermint extract
2 tbsp cocoa powder
½ cup all-purpose flour

White chocolate ganache filling
½ cup whipping cream
6 oz good-quality white chocolate,
chopped
1 tsp peppermint extract
5 oz semisweet chocolate, chopped
3 tbsp unsalted butter

◆ With an electric mixer, beat the butter and sugar until light and creamy, about 3 minutes. Add the egg and beat for 2–3 minutes longer, until the mixture is fluffy. Beat in the peppermint extract.
◆ Sift the cocoa and flour together into a bowl. With a wooden spoon, gradually stir into the creamy butter mixture just until blended. Turn out the dough onto a piece of plastic wrap and use to flatten the dough to a thick disc. Wrap and refrigerate for 1 hour.
◆ Preheat the oven to 350°F. Grease and flour 2 large baking sheets. Remove the dough from the refrigerator and divide in half. Refrigerate one half of dough.
◆ On a lightly floured surface, roll out the other half of the dough to about ⅛ inch thick. Using a floured heart-shaped or flower-shaped cutter, about 2 inches in diameter, cut out as many shapes as possible and place the shapes on prepared baking sheets; reserve any trimmings. Repeat with the second half of the dough.
◆ Bake for 7–8 minutes, until the edges are set; do not overbake as cookies burn easily. Transfer the baking sheets to a wire rack to cool for 10 minutes. With a metal spatula, transfer the cookies to a wire rack to cool completely.
◆ Prepare the filling. In a saucepan over medium heat, bring the cream to the boil. Remove from the heat. Add the white chocolate all at once, stirring constantly until smooth. Stir in the peppermint extract and pour into a bowl. Cool for about 1 hour until firm but not hard.
◆ With a hand-held electric mixer, beat the white chocolate filling for 30–45 seconds, until it becomes lighter and fluffier. Spread a little white chocolate filling onto the bottom of 1 cookie and immediately cover it with another cookie, pressing together gently. Repeat with the remaining cookies and filling. Refrigerate for 30 minutes, or until firm.
◆ In a saucepan over low heat, melt the chocolate and butter, stirring frequently until smooth. Remove from the heat. Cool for 15 minutes until slightly thickened.
◆ Spread a small amount of glaze onto the top of each sandwiched cookie, being careful not to let the glaze drip or spread over the edges. Chill until the glaze is set.

RIGHT *Chocolate-Mint Sandwich Cookies*

Florentines

MAKES ABOUT 8-10

¼ cup butter
¼ cup sugar
¼ cup all-purpose flour, sifted
a scant ½ cup almonds, blanched and
chopped
¼ cup candied peel, chopped
⅛ cup raisins, chopped
⅛ cup maraschino cherries, washed
and chopped
rind of ½ lemon, finely grated
4 oz semisweet chocolate

◆ Preheat the oven to 350°F. Line baking sheets with waxed paper.
◆ Put the butter and sugar into a pan and gently heat them together until melted.
◆ Remove the pan from the heat and stir in the flour.
◆ Add the almonds, candied peel, raisins, cherries, and lemon rind. Stir well.
◆ Put teaspoonfuls of the mixture well apart on the baking sheets.
◆ Bake in the oven for about 10 minutes or until golden brown.
◆ While still warm, press the edges of the cookies back to a neat shape. Leave to cool on the baking sheets until set, then carefully lift onto a wire rack.
◆ Melt the chocolate. Spread over the smooth sides of the florentines. As the chocolate begins to set, mark into wavy lines with a fork. Leave to set.

Triple Decker Squares

MAKES 16

½ cup butter or margarine
¼ cup sugar
1½ cups all-purpose flour

Filling
½ cup butter or margarine
⅓ cup sugar
2 tbsp corn syrup
6 oz can condensed milk

Topping
6 oz semisweet chocolate
2 tbsp milk

◆ Preheat the oven to 350°F. Cream together the butter or margarine and sugar until light and fluffy.
◆ Stir in the flour. Work the dough with your hands and knead well together.
◆ Roll out and press into a shallow 8 inch square pan. Prick well with a fork.
◆ Bake in the oven for 25-30 minutes. Cool in the pan.
◆ To make the filling, put all the ingredients into a pan and heat gently, stirring until the sugar has dissolved. Bring to the boil and cook, stirring for 5-7 minutes until golden.

◆ Pour the caramel over the shortbread base and leave to set.
◆ Melt the chocolate and milk together. Spread it evenly over the caramel. Leave until quite cold before cutting into squares.

Viennese Chocolate Cookies

MAKES ABOUT 20

1 cup butter or margarine
⅛ cup powdered sugar, sifted
2 cups all-purpose flour
4 tbsp drinking chocolate powder
¼ cup cornstarch
4 oz semisweet chocolate
a little powdered sugar

◆ Preheat the oven to 350°F. Cream together the butter or margarine and sugar until light and fluffy.
◆ Work in the flour, drinking chocolate powder, and cornstarch.
◆ Put the mixture into a piping bag fitted with a large star nozzle. Pipe in fingers, or shells, or "s" shapes onto greased baking sheets.
◆ Bake in the oven for 20-25 minutes. Cool on a wire rack.
◆ Melt the chocolate. Dip half of each cookie into the chocolate and leave to set on waxed paper.
◆ Dust the uncoated halves of the cookies with powdered sugar.

VARIATION

To make chocolate gems, pipe mixture into small individual star shapes. Bake for about half the time. Place a chocolate dot in the center of each one while still hot.

$\mathscr{S}$MALL $\mathscr{C}$AKES

Raspberry Chocolate Eclairs   31

Chocolate-Mint Cupcakes   32

Chocolate Meringues   32

Cream Cheese-Marbled Brownies   34

Chocolate and Coconut Sarah Bernhardts   35

Chunky Chocolate Brownies with Fudge Glaze   36

Jaffa Cakes   38

Butterfly Cakes   39

Cocoa Brownies with Milk Chocolate and Walnut Topping   40

Classic Brownies   40

Chocolate Boxes   42

Chocolate Malties   42

Raspberry Chocolate Eclairs

MAKES ABOUT 10

¼ cup butter or margarine,
cut in pieces
¼ cup water
⅝ cup all-purpose flour
2 eggs, beaten

Filling
¼ cup heavy (table) cream
8 oz fresh raspberries
a little sugar

Topping
6 oz semisweet chocolate
2 tbsp butter

◆ Preheat the oven to 400°F. Put the butter or margarine and water into a pan and bring to the boil.
◆ Remove from the heat and tip all the flour into the pan at once. Beat with a wooden spoon until the paste forms a ball. Cool.
◆ Whisk the eggs into the paste, a little at a time. Continue beating until the mixture is glossy.
◆ Put the pastry into a piping bag fitted with a large plain nozzle. Pipe 3 inch lengths onto greased baking sheets.
◆ Bake in the oven for about 25 minutes, until golden brown.

◆ Remove from the oven and make a couple of slits in the sides of each one to allow steam to escape. Return to the oven for a few minutes to dry. Cool on a wire rack.
◆ To make the filling, whisk the cream until stiff. Fold in the raspberries and sugar to taste.
◆ Make a slit down the side of each eclair and fill with the cream mixture.
◆ Melt together the chocolate and butter. Dip the tops of the eclairs into the chocolate and then leave to set.

Chocolate-Mint Cup Cakes

MAKES ABOUT 18-20

2 cups all-purpose or cake flour
1 tsp bicarbonate of soda
¼ tsp salt
4 tbsp cocoa powder
⅔ cup butter, softened
1¼ cups fine granulated sugar
3 eggs
2 tsp peppermint extract
1 cup milk

Chocolate-mint glaze
3 oz semisweet chocolate
¼ cup butter
1 tsp peppermint extract

◆ Preheat the oven to 350°F. Line 20 deep muffin pans with cupcake papers.
◆ Sift together the flour, bicarbonate of soda, salt, and cocoa powder.
◆ In a second large bowl, using an electric mixer, beat the butter and sugar until light and creamy, about 5 minutes. Add the eggs, 1 at a time, beating well after each addition, then beat in the mint extract.
◆ On low speed, beat in the flour and cocoa mixture alternately with the milk just until blended. Spoon into cupcake papers, filling each pan about three-quarters full.

◆ Bake for 12-15 minutes, until a fine skewer inserted in the center comes out clean; do not overbake. Cool in the tins on a wire rack for 5 minutes; remove the cakes to wire rack to cool completely.
◆ Meanwhile, prepare the glaze. In a saucepan over low heat, melt the chocolate and butter, stirring until smooth. Remove from the heat and stir in the mint extract. Cool until spreadable, then spread on top of each cake.

RIGHT *Chocolate-Mint Cup Cakes*

Chocolate Meringues

MAKES 6-8

3 egg whites
⅓ cup fine granulated sugar
⅓ cup powdered sugar, sifted
2 tbsp unsweetened cocoa powder, sifted

Filling
¼ cup heavy cream
1 tbsp granulated brown sugar
2 tsp unsweetened cocoa powder

◆ Preheat the oven to 225°F. Beat the egg whites until they form stiff peaks. Gradually whisk in the fine granulated sugar, a little at a time.
◆ Whisk in the powdered sugar.
◆ Fold in the cocoa powder.
◆ Put the mixture into a piping bag fitted with a large star nozzle. Line baking sheets with waxed paper.
◆ Pipe the mixture into spirals.

◆ Bake in the oven for 2-3 hours or until the meringues are dry. Cool on a wire rack.
◆ Whip the cream until stiff. Stir in the sugar and cocoa. Sandwich the meringues together, two at a time, with the chocolate cream.

Cream Cheese-Marbled Brownies

MAKES 15-20

9 oz bitter chocolate, chopped
1 cup unsalted butter, softened
1 cup granulated sugar
⅓ cup granulated brown sugar
3 eggs
1 tbsp vanilla extract
1 cup all-purpose flour
¼ tsp salt
1 lb cream cheese, softened
1 egg
1 tsp vanilla extract
finely grated rind of 1 lemon

◆ Preheat the oven to 350°F. Invert a 9 x 13 inch cake pan and mold foil over the bottom. Turn the pan over and line with the foil; leave the foil to extend above the sides of the tin. Grease the bottom and sides of the foil.

◆ In a saucepan over low heat, melt the chocolate and ½ cup of the butter, stirring frequently until smooth. Remove from the heat. Cool to room temperature.

◆ In a bowl, using a hand-held mixer, beat the remaining butter, ⅔ cup granulated sugar and the brown sugar until light and creamy, 2-3 minutes. Add the eggs, 1 at a time, beating well after each addition. Beat in the vanilla extract, then slowly beat in the melted chocolate and butter. Stir in the flour and salt just until blended.

◆ In a bowl, using a hand-held electric mixer, beat the cream cheese and remaining sugar until smooth, about 1 minute. Beat in the egg, vanilla extract and lemon rind.

◆ Pour two-thirds of the brownie batter into the pan and spread evenly. Pour the cream cheese mixture over the brownie layer. Spoon the remaining brownie mixture in dollops on top of the cream cheese mixture in 2 rows along the long side of the pan. Using a knife or spoon, swirl the brownie batter into the cream cheese batter to create a marble effect.

◆ Bake for 25-35 minutes, or until a toothpick inserted 2 inches from the edge of the pan comes out with just a few crumbs attached. Transfer to a wire rack to cool in the pan.

◆ When cool, use the foil to help lift the brownie out of the pan. Invert onto another rack or baking sheet and peel off the foil. Invert back onto the wire rack and slide onto a serving plate. Cut into squares and wrap and refrigerate; or wrap until ready to serve, then cut into squares.

Chocolate and Coconut Sarah Bernhardts

MAKES ABOUT 16

3½ oz shredded coconut
⅓ cup sugar
2 tbsp all-purpose flour
3 tbsp cocoa powder
1 tsp vanilla extract
1 tbsp corn syrup
2-3 egg whites

Ganache topping
¼ cup cream
8 oz semisweet chocolate, chopped
⅛ cup pieces unsalted butter
2 tbsp shredded coconut

Chocolate glaze
6 oz semisweet chocolate, chopped
⅛ cup pieces unsalted butter
1 tbsp corn syrup

◆ First prepare the topping. In a medium saucepan over medium heat, bring the cream to the boil. Remove from the heat. Add the chocolate all at once, stirring well until melted and smooth. Beat in the butter. Cool, then refrigerate for 1-2 hours, until thickened and chilled, but not set.

◆ Preheat the oven to 325°F. Line a large baking sheet with foil and grease the foil. In a bowl, combine the coconut, sugar, flour, and cocoa powder. Stir in the vanilla and corn syrup and 2 egg whites; if the mixture is too dry, add the third egg white, little by little, until a thick dough-like batter forms and holds together.

◆ Using a miniature ice cream scoop, about 1 inch in diameter, or a teaspoon, place 16 scoops onto the baking sheet. With your forefinger, flatten each scoop, making a slight indentation in the center of each.

◆ Bake for 12-14 minutes, just until the macaroons are set on the outside. Do not overbake or they will be too hard. Cool on the baking sheet for 10-15 minutes, then remove from the foil to a wire rack to cool completely.

◆ When the topping mixture is cold and thick, beat with an electric mixer for 30-45 seconds, just until the mixture lightens in colour and thickens enough to pipe; do not overbeat or the mixture will become grainy.

◆ Quickly spoon the mixture into a large piping bag fitted with a ½ inch plain nozzle and pipe a 1 inch mound on top of each macaroon, pressing the tip firmly onto the center. Chill for 1-2 hours, until the topping is firm.

◆ Prepare the glaze. In a small saucepan over a low heat, melt the chocolate and butter with corn syrup, stirring frequently until smooth. Pour into a tall, narrow container, mug or strong paper cup to allow for easy dipping. Cool the chocolate.

◆ Holding each macaroon by the very bottom edge, carefully and quickly dip into the chocolate glaze to cover the filling and top of each macaroon to within about ¼ inch of the bottom, twisting and swirling in chocolate glaze so the entire macaroon is coated. Leave the excess to drip off, then quickly turn upright and place on a baking sheet. Decorate the tops with a sprinkling of coconut.

Chunky Chocolate Brownies with Fudge Glaze

MAKES 14–16

10 oz bitter chocolate, chopped
¼ cup unsalted butter, cut into pieces
½ cup brown sugar
¼ cup granulated sugar
2 eggs
1 tbsp vanilla extract
½ cup all-purpose flour
¼ cup pecans or walnuts, chopped and toasted
5 oz good-quality white chocolate, chopped into ¼ inch pieces

Fudgy chocolate glaze
6 oz semisweet chocolate, chopped
¼ cup unsalted butter, cut into pieces
2 tbsp corn syrup
2 tsp vanilla extract
1 tsp instant coffee powder

◆ Preheat the oven to 350°F. Invert an 8 inch square cake pan and mold a piece of foil over the bottom. Turn the pan over and line with the molded foil. Lightly grease foil.

◆ In a saucepan over low heat, melt the chocolate and butter, stirring frequently until smooth. Remove the pan from the heat.

◆ Stir in the sugars and continue stirring for 2 minutes longer, until the sugar is dissolved. Beat in the eggs and vanilla extract. Stir in the flour until blended. Stir in the nuts and chopped chocolate. Pour into the lined pan.

◆ Bake for 20-25 minutes, until a toothpick inserted 2 inches from the center comes out with just a few crumbs attached; do not overbake. Transfer to a wire rack to cool for 30 minutes. Using the foil as a guide, remove the brownie from the pan and cool on the rack for at least 2 hours.

◆ Prepare the glaze. In a saucepan over medium heat, melt the

chocolate, butter, corn syrup, vanilla extract, and coffee powder, stirring frequently until smooth. Remove from the heat. Refrigerate for 1 hour, or until thickened and spreadable.

◆ Invert the brownie onto a plate and remove the foil. Invert back onto the rack and slide onto a serving platter, top-side up. Using a metal spatula, spread a thick layer of glaze over the top of the brownie just to the edges. Refrigerate for 1 hour, until set. Cut into squares or bars.

Jaffa Cakes

MAKES 18

2 eggs
¼ cup sugar
⅜ cup self-rising flour, sifted
approximately 4 tbsp marmalade, sieved
4 oz semisweet chocolate
rind of ¼ orange, finely grated
2 tsp corn oil
1 tbsp water

◆ Preheat the oven to 400°F. Put the eggs and sugar into a bowl. Whisk until thick and creamy so that when the whisk is lifted the mixture leaves a trail. If using a hand whisk, put the bowl over a pan of hot water.
◆ With a metal spoon, fold in the flour.
◆ Spoon the mixture into about 18 well-greased, round-bottomed muffin pans. Bake for about 10 minutes until golden brown.
◆ Remove and cool on a wire rack.
◆ Spread a little marmalade over each cake.

◆ Put the chocolate, orange rind, oil, and water into a bowl over a pan of hot water. Stir well until melted. Cool until the chocolate starts to thicken and then spoon over the marmalade. Leave to set.

Butterfly Cakes

MAKES 14-16

½ cup butter or margarine
½ cup sugar
2 eggs
1 tsp grated orange rind
2 oz semisweet chocolate, finely grated
1 cup self-rising flour

Frosting
⅓ cup butter or margarine
⅞ cup powdered sugar, sifted
3 oz semisweet chocolate, melted

To decorate
powdered sugar
seedless raspberry jam or
maraschino cherries

◆ Preheat the oven to 350°F. Put the butter or margarine and sugar into a bowl and cream together until light and fluffy.
◆ Beat in the eggs a little at a time. Stir in the orange rind and chocolate.
◆ Fold in the flour.
◆ Arrange cupcake papers in a metal muffin pan. Divide the mixture between the papers.
◆ Bake in the oven for about 15-20 minutes. Cool.
◆ To make the frosting, cream together the butter and powdered sugar. Gradually beat in the cooled, melted chocolate.

◆ Starting ¼ inch in from the edge, remove the top of each cake by cutting in and slightly down to form a cavity.
◆ Pipe a little frosting in the cavity of each cake.
◆ Sprinkle the reserved cake tops with powdered sugar and cut each one in half. Place each half, cut side outwards, onto the frosting to form wings.
◆ Pipe small rosettes of frosting in the center of each cake. Top with a small blob of raspberry jam or half a maraschino cherry.

Cocoa Brownies with Milk Chocolate and Walnut Topping

MAKES 12

½ cup all-purpose flour
3 tbsp cocoa powder
¼ tsp baking powder
¼ tsp salt
½ cup unsalted butter
1 cup sugar
2 eggs
2 tsp vanilla extract
generous ½ cup walnuts, coarsely
chopped

Milk chocolate and walnut topping
6-7 oz milk chocolate
generous ½ cup walnuts, chopped

◆ Preheat the oven to 350°F. Grease a 9 inch springform pan or 9 inch cake pan with a removable bottom.

Into a bowl sift the flour, cocoa powder, baking powder, and salt. Set aside.
◆ In a medium saucepan over medium heat, melt the butter. Stir in the sugar and remove from the heat, stirring 2-3 minutes to dissolve the sugar. Beat in the eggs and vanilla extract. Stir in the flour mixture just until blended; then stir in the walnuts. Pour into the prepared pan, smoothing the top evenly.
◆ Bake for 18-24 minutes, until a toothpick inserted 2 inches from the center comes out with just a few crumbs attached; do not overbake or the brownie will be dry.
◆ Prepare the topping. Break the milk chocolate into pieces. As soon as the brownie tests done, remove from the oven to a heatproof surface. Quickly place the chocolate pieces all

over the top of the brownie; do not let the chocolate touch the side of the pan. Return to the oven for 20-30 seconds.
◆ Remove the brownie and, with the back of a spoon, gently spread the softened chocolate evenly over the top. Sprinkle walnuts evenly over the top and, with the back of a spoon, gently press them into the chocolate. Cool on a wire rack for 30 minutes.
◆ Refrigerate for 1 hour, until set. Run a knife around the edge of the pan to loosen the brownie from the edge. Carefully remove the side of the pan. Cool completely and serve at room temperature.

RIGHT *Cocoa Brownies with Milk Chocolate and Walnut Topping*

Classic Brownies

MAKES ABOUT 20

1½ cups granulated brown sugar
4 tbsp unsweetened cocoa powder,
sifted
¼ cup self-rising flour
2 eggs
2 tbsp milk
½ cup butter, melted
scant ½ cup walnuts, finely chopped
¼ cup raisins, chopped
walnut halves, to decorate

Frosting
4 oz semisweet chocolate
1 tbsp black coffee

◆ Preheat the oven to 350°F. Mix together the sugar, cocoa and flour.
◆ Beat together the eggs and milk. Stir into the flour mixture, together with the butter, walnuts and raisins.
◆ Spread in a greased and base-lined pan measuring 7 x 11 x 1½ inches.
◆ Bake in the oven for about 30 minutes. Cool.
◆ Melt the chocolate and coffee together. Spread over the cake.
◆ To serve, decorate with walnut halves. Cut into squares when cold.

Chocolate Boxes

MAKES 9

1 egg
2 tbsp sugar
¼ cup all-purpose flour

Filling
¼ pt water
5 oz pkt tangerine jello
1 cup curd cheese
1¼ cups heavy cream
2 tbsp apricot jam, sieved

To decorate
36 x 2 inch chocolate squares
(see page 18)
whipped cream
9 mandarin orange segments
quartered walnuts

RIGHT *Chocolate Boxes*

◆ Preheat the oven to 400°F. Whisk the egg and sugar together until the mixture is thick and creamy and the whisk leaves a trail when lifted.
◆ Using a metal spoon, gently fold in the flour. Pour into a shallow greased and base-lined 7 inch square pan.
◆ Bake for 10-12 minutes. Turn out and cool.
◆ Heat the water. Add the jello and stir until dissolved. Chill until the mixture begins to turn syrupy.
◆ Beat the cheese and gradually add the jello.
◆ Whip the cream until thick and fold into the cheese mixture. Pour into a 7 inch square cake pan, lined with waxed paper. Chill until set.
◆ Spread the sponge with apricot jam. Unmold the cheese mixture onto the sponge. Trim the edges.

◆ Cut the cake into nine squares. Press a chocolate square onto each side of each cake.
◆ To serve, pipe whipped cream on top of each chocolate box. Top with mandarins and walnuts.

VARIATIONS
◆ Use cherry jello, cherry jam and top with canned or fresh cherries.
◆ Use strawberry/raspberry jello, strawberry/raspberry jam and top with fresh strawberries/raspberries.
◆ Use lemon jello, lemon cheese and top with pieces of canned or fresh pineapple.
◆ Use lime jello, lime marmalade and top with halved slices of kiwi fruit.

Chocolate Malties

MAKES ABOUT 20-24

3 oz semisweet chocolate
a scant ½ cup cream cheese
¼ cup butter or margarine
1 oz instant malted milk powder
½ tsp vanilla extract
2¼ cups powdered sugar, sifted
7 tbsp milk
1¼ cups self-rising flour
½ tsp baking powder
⅛ cup softened butter or margarine
2 eggs
¼ cup milk
chocolate dots, to decorate

◆ Preheat the oven to 350°F. Melt the chocolate and allow to cool slightly.
◆ Beat together the cream cheese, butter or margarine, malted milk powder, and vanilla extract.
◆ Beat in the powdered sugar and half the milk alternately. Beat in the melted chocolate.
◆ Remove 1 cup of the chocolate mixture. Cover and reserve for the frosting.
◆ Sift together the flour and baking powder.
◆ Beat the softened butter into the chocolate mixture.
◆ Beat in the eggs.
◆ Stir in the flour alternately with the remaining milk.
◆ Put cupcake papers into muffin pans and fill two-thirds full with the mixture.

◆ Bake in the oven for about 20 minutes. Cool.
◆ To serve, frost the cakes with the reserved chocolate icing. Decorate with chocolate dots if you wish.

Large Cakes and Gateaux

Triple Chocolate Cheesecake

SERVES 18-20

8 oz semisweet chocolate wholewheat
cookies
¼ cup butter, melted
½ tsp ground cinnamon

Filling
1 lb semisweet chocolate, chopped
¼ cup butter, cut into pieces
1 cup sour cream
2 lb cream cheese, softened
1 cup sugar
5 eggs
1 tbsp vanilla extract

Chocolate glaze
4 oz semisweet chocolate, chopped
½ cup heavy cream
1 tsp vanilla extract
cocoa powder

◆ Preheat the oven to 350°F. Lightly grease the bottom and sides of a 10 inch, 3 inch deep springform pan.
◆ Prepare the crust. In a food processor, process the chocolate cookies until fine crumbs form. Pour in the melted butter and cinnamon. Process just until blended. Pat onto the bottom and to within ½ inch of the top of the sides of the pan.
◆ Bake for 5-7 minutes, just until set. Remove to a wire rack to cool while you prepare the filling. Lower the oven temperature to 325°F.
◆ Prepare the filling. In a saucepan over low heat, melt the chocolate and butter, stirring frequently until smooth. Set aside to cool; stir in the sour cream.
◆ With an electric mixer, beat the cream cheese and sugar until smooth, 2-4 minutes. Add the eggs, 1 at a time, beating well after each addition, scraping the bowl occasionally. Slowly beat in the chocolate mixture and vanilla extract just until blended. Pour into the baked crust. Place the pan on a baking sheet; place a small saucepan of water on the floor of the oven to create moisture.
◆ Bake for 1-1½ hours, or until the edge of the cheesecake is set but the center is still slightly soft. Turn off the oven but leave the cheesecake in the oven for another 30 minutes. Remove to a wire rack to cool. Run a knife around the edge of the cheesecake in the pan to separate it from the side; this helps to prevent cracking. Cool to room temperature.
◆ Prepare the glaze. In a saucepan, melt the chocolate with the cream and vanilla extract, stirring until smooth. Cool and leave to thicken slightly, 10-15 minutes. Pour over the warm cake in the pan; cool the glazed cake completely. Using strips of waxed paper dust cocoa in horizontal bands across the top of the cake. Refrigerate, loosely covered, overnight.
◆ To serve, run a knife around the edge of the pan to loosen the cheesecake. Remove the side of the pan. If you like, slide a knife under the crust to separate the cheesecake from the base, and, with a metal spatula, slide it onto a serving platter.

Chocolate and Banana Swirl Cheesecake

SERVES 16

Crumb crust

5 oz ginger snaps
¼ cup walnuts
¼ cup butter, melted
½ tsp ground ginger

Filling

4 oz semisweet chocolate, chopped
¼ cup butter, cut into pieces
2½ lb cream cheese, softened
1¼ cups sugar
1 tbsp vanilla extract
5 eggs
1 cup sour cream
3 ripe bananas
1 tbsp lemon juice

◆ Preheat the oven to 350°F. Lightly grease a 10 inch, 3 inch deep springform pan.

◆ In a food processor, process the ginger snaps and walnuts until fine crumbs form. Pour in the melted butter and ginger. Process just until blended. Pat onto the bottom and to within ½ inch of the top of the sides of the pan.

◆ Bake for 5-7 minutes, just until set. Remove to a wire rack to cool while preparing the filling. Lower the oven temperature to 300°F.

◆ In a saucepan over a low heat, melt the chocolate and butter, stirring frequently until smooth. Set aside to cool.

◆ With an electric mixer, beat the cream cheese and sugar until smooth, 2-4 minutes; stir in the vanilla extract. Add the eggs, 1 at a time, beating well after each addition, scraping the bowl occasionally, then blend in the sour cream. Pour about 1½ cups of cream cheese mixture into a bowl and stir in the melted chocolate until well blended. Set the mixture aside.

◆ In a second bowl, mash the bananas with the lemon juice, then beat into the remaining cream cheese mixture until well blended.

◆ Pour the banana mixture into the baked crust. Drop spoonfuls of chocolate mixture over the banana mixture in a circle about 1 inch from the sides of the pan. With a spoon or knife, swirl the chocolate mixture into the banana mixture, creating a marbled effect. Do not overmix. Place the pan on a baking sheet; place a small saucepan of water on the floor of the oven to create moisture during baking.

◆ Bake for 50-60 minutes, until the edge of the cheesecake is set, but the center is still soft. Turn off the oven and leave to stand for 30 minutes; this helps to prevent cracking. Transfer to a wire rack, run a knife around the edge of the cheesecake in the pan to separate it from the sides; this also helps to prevent cracking. Cool completely, then refrigerate, loosely covered, overnight.

◆ To serve, run a knife around the edge of the pan to loosen the cheesecake. Remove the side of the pan. If you like, slide a knife under the crust to separate the cheesecake from the base, then, with a metal spatula, slide onto a serving platter. Alternatively, leave the cheesecake on the pan base to avoid breaking the crust or surface and serve from the pan base.

White Chocolate Cheesecake

SERVES 16-20

Crumb crust
5 oz wholewheat cookies
¼ cup pecan or walnut halves
¼ cup butter, melted
½ tsp ground cinnamon

Filling
12 oz good-quality white chocolate, chopped
½ cup whipping cream
1½ lb cream cheese
⅓ cup sugar
4 eggs
1 tbsp vanilla extract

To decorate
cocoa powder for dusting (optional)
white and dark chocolate curls (see page 18)

Sour cream topping
2 cups sour cream
¼ cup sugar
1 tsp vanilla extract

◆ Preheat the oven to 350°F. Lightly grease a 9 inch, 3 inch deep springform pan.

◆ Prepare the crust. In a food processor, process the cookies and nuts until fine crumbs form. Pour in the melted butter and cinnamon. Process just until blended. Pat onto the bottom and to within ½ inch of the top of the sides of the pan.

◆ Bake for 5-7 minutes, just until set. Remove to a wire rack to cool while you prepare the filling. Lower the oven temperature to 300°F.

◆ Prepare the filling. In a saucepan over a low heat, melt the chocolate with the cream, stirring frequently until smooth. Set aside to cool.

◆ With an electric mixer, beat the cream cheese and sugar until smooth, 2-4 minutes. Add the eggs, 1 at a time, beating well after each addition, scraping the bowl occasionally. Slowly beat in the white chocolate mixture and vanilla extract just until blended. Pour into the baked crust. Place on a baking sheet; place a small saucepan of water on the floor of the oven to create moisture during baking.

◆ Bake for 45-55 minutes, or until the edge of the cheesecake is firm but the center is still slightly soft. Remove the cheesecake to a wire rack. Increase the oven temperature to 400°F.

◆ Prepare the topping. In a bowl, beat the sour cream, sugar, and vanilla extract. Pour over the cheesecake and return to the oven. Bake for 5 minutes longer. Transfer to a wire rack to cool to room temperature. Run a knife around the edge of the cake in the pan to separate it from the side; this helps to prevent cracking. Cool completely, then refrigerate overnight.

◆ To serve, run a knife around the edge of the pan to loosen the cheesecake. Remove the side of the pan. If you like, slide the knife under the crust to separate the cheesecake from the base then, with a metal spatula, slide onto a serving platter. Alternatively, leave the cheesecake on the pan base to avoid breaking the crust or surface and serve from the pan base.

◆ Dust the top of the cheesecake with cocoa or decorate with white and dark chocolate curls.

White Chocolate and Coconut Layer Cake

SERVES 12-16

*4 oz good-quality white chocolate,
chopped*
½ cup whipping cream
½ cup milk
1 tbsp light rum
½ cup unsalted butter, softened
¼ cup sugar
3 eggs
2 cups cake flour
1 tsp baking powder
pinch of salt
½ cup shredded sweetened coconut

White chocolate mousse
*15 oz good-quality white chocolate,
chopped*
4½ cups whipping cream
½ cup light rum
fresh coconut strips for decoration

◆ Preheat the oven to 350°F. Grease and flour 9 inch round, 2 inch deep cake pans.
◆ In the top of a double boiler over a low heat, melt the chocolate with the cream, stirring until smooth. Stir in the milk and rum; set aside to cool.
◆ With an electric mixer, beat the butter with the sugar until pale and thick, about 5 minutes. Add the eggs, 1 at a time, beating well after each addition. In another bowl, stir together the flour, baking powder and salt. Alternately add the flour mixture and melted white chocolate in batches, just until blended; stir in half the coconut. Pour the batter into the pans and spread evenly.
◆ Bake for 20-25 minutes, until a toothpick inserted in the centers comes out clean. Cool on a wire rack for 10 minutes. Unmold the cakes onto the wire rack and cool completely.
◆ Meanwhile, prepare the mousse. In a saucepan over a low heat, melt the white chocolate and 1½ cups cream, stirring frequently until smooth. Stir in the rum, then pour into a bowl. Refrigerate for 1-1½ hours, until completely cold and thickened.
◆ Whip the remaining cream until soft peaks form. Stir 1 spoonful of cream into the mousse mixture to lighten, then fold in about 1 cup whipped cream.

◆ With a serrated knife, slice the cake layers in half horizontally, making 4 layers. Place 1 layer on a plate and spread one-sixth of the mousse on top. Sprinkle with one-third of the remaining coconut. Place a second layer on top and spread with one-sixth of mousse. Sprinkle with another third of coconut. Place a third layer on top and spread with another one-sixth of mousse and the remaining coconut. Cover with the last cake layer and cover the top and sides with the remaining mousse.
◆ Spread the remaining whipped cream over the top and sides of the cake and garnish with fresh coconut strips.

SWEET SUCCESS

If fresh coconut is unavailable, use shredded sweetened coconut for garnish. Spread ⅛ cup coconut on baking sheet and bake at 350°F for 10-12 minutes, stirring twice, until golden. Press into the sides and sprinkle on the top of the cake.

For fresh coconut strips, use a swivel-bladed vegetable peeler to make paper-thin strips from fresh coconut pieces. Leave the brown skin on the pieces to create a pretty edge.

Family Chocolate Cake

SERVES 8-10

3 oz semisweet chocolate
¼ cup clear honey
½ cup butter or margarine
¼ cup sugar
2 eggs
1¼ cups self-rising flour
¼ cup unsweetened cocoa powder
1½ level tsp baking powder
¼ tsp vanilla extract
¼ cup milk

Frosting
2 oz semisweet chocolate
3 tbsp water
⅛ cup butter
1¼ cups powdered sugar, sifted

◆ Preheat the oven to 350°F. Put the chocolate and honey into a small bowl over a pan of hot water. Stir until the chocolate has melted. Cool.
◆ Cream together the butter or margarine and sugar until light and fluffy.
◆ Beat in the chocolate mixture, then the eggs.
◆ Sift together the flour, cocoa powder, and baking powder.
◆ Stir in the flour mixture a little at a time, alternately with the vanilla extract and milk.
◆ Pour the mixture into a lined 7½ inch round cake pan.
◆ Bake in the oven for about 45 minutes.

◆ Turn onto a wire rack, leaving the lining paper on the cake to form a collar.
◆ When the cake is cool, make the frosting. Put the chocolate and water into a small saucepan and melt over a gentle heat.
◆ Remove from the heat and stir in the butter. When the butter has melted, beat in the powdered sugar.
◆ Spread the frosting over the top of the cake and swirl with a metal spatula. When the frosting is firm, remove the lining paper from the cake.

Saucy Chocolate Cake

SERVES 8

1 cup cake flour
½ cup sugar
5 tbsp cocoa powder
2 tsp baking powder
½ tsp salt
¼ cup milk
⅛ cup butter
1 tsp vanilla extract

Topping
¼ cup light brown sugar
½ cup chopped pecans (optional)
1¼ cups boiling water
powdered sugar for dusting

◆ Preheat the oven to 350°F. Lightly butter an 8 x 8 x 2 inch baking pan.
◆ Combine the flour, sugar, 3 tbsp of cocoa powder, baking powder, and salt. Stir in the milk, butter, and vanilla extract just until blended. Spoon into the pan and spread evenly.
◆ In another bowl, combine the brown sugar, chopped nuts, and remaining cocoa; gradually stir in the boiling water until the sugar dissolves. Gently pour over the batter in the baking pan.
◆ Bake for 25-30 minutes, until the top of the cake springs back when touched with a fingertip. Cool for 30-40 minutes on a wire rack. Dust with powdered sugar and serve warm or chilled.

Chocolate Pecan Torte

SERVES 16

7 oz semisweet chocolate, chopped
½ cup pieces unsalted butter
4 eggs
½ cup sugar
2 tsp vanilla extract
¼ cup ground pecans
24 pecan halves

Chocolate honeyglaze
4 oz semisweet chocolate, chopped
¼ cup pieces unsalted butter
2 tbsp honey

SWEET SUCCESS

This cake can be baked 2-3 days ahead, wrapped tightly and refrigerated or even frozen. Bring to room temperature before glazing.

◆ Preheat the oven to 350°F. Grease a 8 inch, 2 inch deep springform pan; line the bottom with waxed paper and grease the paper. Wrap the bottom of the pan in foil.
◆ In a saucepan over a low heat, melt the chocolate and butter, stirring until smooth. Remove from the heat.
◆ With an electric mixer, beat the eggs with sugar and vanilla extract just until frothy, 1-2 minutes. Stir in the melted chocolate and ground nuts until well blended. Pour into the pan and tap gently on a work surface to break any large air bubbles.
◆ Place the pan into a larger roasting pan and pour boiling water into the roasting pan, about ¾ inch up the side of the springform pan. Bake for 25-30 minutes, until the edge of the cake is set, but the center is still soft. Remove the pan from the water-bath and remove the foil. Cool on a wire rack completely.

◆ Meanwhile, place the pecan halves on a baking sheet and bake for 10-12 minutes, until just brown, stirring occasionally.
◆ In a saucepan over a low heat, melt the chocolate, butter, and honey, stirring until smooth; remove from the heat. Carefully dip the roasted nuts halfway into the glaze and place on a waxed paper-lined baking sheet until set. The glaze will have thickened slightly.
◆ Remove the side of the pan and turn the cake onto a wire rack placed over a baking sheet to catch any drips. Remove the pan bottom and paper so the bottom of cake is now the top. Pour the thickened glaze over the cake, tilting the rack slightly to spread the glaze. If necessary, use a metal spatula to smooth the sides. Arrange the nuts around the outside edge of the torte and leave the glaze to set. With a metal spatula, carefully slide the cake onto a serving dish.

Dobos Torte

SERVES 8

6 eggs, separated
rind of 1 lemon, grated
¼ cup sugar
1¼ cups cake flour, sifted

Butter cream
8 oz semisweet chocolate
1 cup butter
3 cups powdered sugar, sifted

Caramel
¼ cup granulated sugar

◆ Preheat the oven to 400°F. Grease and flour 7 flat surfaces, such as baking sheets and roasting pans. Using a cake pan or plate, mark a circle 8 inches in diameter on each one.

◆ Whisk the egg yolks with the lemon rind and sugar in a mixing bowl until the mixture is thick.

◆ Whisk the egg whites until stiff.

◆ Fold the egg whites and flour alternately into the egg yolk mixture.

◆ Divide the mixture evenly between the circles. Bake in batches in the oven for about 8 minutes, or until golden brown. Lift onto wire racks to cool.

◆ Use the 8 inch cake pan or plate to trim the edges so that all the circles are the same size.

◆ To make the butter cream, melt the chocolate. Add the butter and stir until melted. Cool. Beat in the sifted powdered sugar.

◆ To make the caramel, put the sugar into a heavy saucepan. Heat very slowly over a low heat, stirring until the sugar is completely dissolved. Heat until the caramel turns golden brown.

◆ Pour the caramel immediately onto one of the cake layers. Before the caramel sets, cut the cake layer into 8 sections, using an oiled or buttered knife.

◆ Sandwich the remaining cake layers together with some of the chocolate butter cream. Spread butter cream round the sides of the cake.

◆ Put the remaining butter cream into a piping bag, fitted with a star nozzle. Pipe eight long whirls on top of the cake, radiating out from the center. Set a caramel-coated section, tilted slightly, on each whirl.

Chocolate and Raspberry Torte

SERVES 10

4 oz semisweet chocolate, chopped
1 cup ground blanched almonds
¼ cup cake flour
½ cup butter, softened
½ cup sugar
4 eggs, separated
¼ tsp cream of tartar

Chocolate and raspberry ganache
frosting and filling
1 cup heavy cream
1 cup seedless raspberry jam
10 oz semisweet chocolate, chopped
⅛ cup butter, cut into pieces
5 tbsp raspberry-flavor liqueur
½ lb fresh raspberries, 8 or 10 reserved
to decorate
chocolate leaves (see page 19) to
decorate

VARIATION

For a lighter look, beat the icing with a hand-held beater for 30-45 seconds until light and fluffy. Immediately frost and decorate the torte before the frosting hardens.

◆ Preheat the oven to 350°F. Grease the bottom and sides of a 15½ x 10½ x 1 inch jelly roll pan. Line the bottom with waxed paper, allowing 1 inch overhang; grease and flour the paper.

◆ In the top of a double boiler over a low heat, melt the chocolate, stirring frequently until smooth. Set aside to cool.

◆ In a bowl, mix the ground almonds and flour until blended. In another bowl, with an electric mixer, beat the butter and half the sugar until pale and creamy, about 3 minutes. Add the egg yolks, 1 at a time, beating well after each addition. Slowly beat in the melted chocolate until well blended, scraping the bowl occasionally.

◆ In a large bowl, with an electric mixer, beat the egg whites with the cream of tartar until stiff peaks form. Gradually sprinkle the remaining sugar over the egg whites in 2 batches, beating until the egg whites are stiff and glossy.

◆ Stir 1 spoonful of egg whites into the chocolate mixture to lighten, then fold in the remaining egg whites and the almond and flour mixture alternately just until blended. Spoon into the pan, spreading evenly.

◆ Bake for 10-12 minutes, or until the cake springs back when touched with a fingertip.

◆ Cool the cake in the pan on a wire rack for 10 minutes. Using the paper corners as a guide, lift the cake out of the pan onto the rack to cool completely.

◆ Meanwhile, prepare the frosting. In a saucepan, bring the cream and half

the raspberry jam to the boil. Remove from the heat and immediately stir in the chocolate until melted and smooth. Beat in the butter and half the raspberry-flavor liqueur. Cool the frosting mixture, then refrigerate until it reaches a spreading consistency, about 1 hour; stir occasionally.

◆ Turn the cake onto a work surface, bottom side up. Trim the cake edges and cut the cake crosswise into 3 equal strips. In a saucepan, melt the remaining jam and raspberry-flavor liqueur, stirring until smooth; spoon equally over each cake strip and leave to soak in, 2-3 minutes.

◆ Place 1 cake strip on a wire rack over a baking sheet to catch the drips. Spread with about 1 cup chilled frosting. Sprinkle with half the raspberries. Top with the second cake strip and spread with 1 cup frosting and remaining raspberries. Place the third cake strip on top, top side up. With a metal spatula, spread the remaining frosting over the top and sides of the torte. Leave to set.

◆ With a metal spatula, slide the torte onto a serving dish. Decorate the top of the torte with chocolate leaves and the reserved raspberries.

Sachertorte

SERVES 8

8 oz semisweet chocolate
½ cup unsalted butter
¼ cup fine granulated sugar
5 eggs, separated
¼ cup ground filberts or almonds
½ cup self-rising flour, sifted

Filling
¼ cup heavy cream, whipped

Frosting
8 oz semisweet chocolate
½ cup butter, melted

To decorate
whipped cream
whole filberts
chocolate leaves (see page 19)

◆ Preheat the oven to 350°F. Melt the chocolate in a bowl over a saucepan of hot water. Add the butter, cut into small pieces, and beat until the butter has melted and the mixture is smooth.

◆ Beat in the sugar. Gradually add the egg yolks, beating well between each addition.

◆ Whisk the egg whites until stiff. Gently fold into the chocolate, with the ground nuts and flour.

◆ Put the mixture into two greased and base-lined 8 inch sandwich cake pans. Bake for 20-25 minutes. Cool on a wire rack.

◆ When the cakes are cold, sandwich together with whipped cream.

◆ To make the frosting, melt the chocolate and gradually add the butter, beating well between each addition. Leave for 20-30 minutes, until cold, and of a coating consistency.

◆ Spread the frosting over the top and sides of the cake. Leave until set.

◆ Decorate with piped whipped cream, filberts and chocolate leaves.

Torta Sorentina (Easter Cake)

SERVES 8

1 cup unsalted butter
4 large eggs
1 cup sugar
2 cups self-rising flour
rind of ½ lemon, grated

Lemon filling
1 egg white
½ cup powdered sugar
½ cup unsalted butter
rind of ½ lemon, grated

Frosting
6 oz semisweet chocolate
2 tbsp cream
⅛ cup butter
candied lemon slices, to decorate

◆ Preheat the oven to 350°F. Melt the butter and leave to cool.
◆ Put the eggs and sugar into a bowl over a pan of hot water and whisk until they are pale and thick and the whisk leaves a trail.
◆ Gently fold in the flour, lemon rind, and butter. Do not overmix.
◆ Pour into a greased and floured 2 qt ring mold. Bake in the oven for 30-40 minutes. Cool slightly, then turn out onto a wire rack.
◆ To make the filling, put the egg white and powdered sugar into a bowl over a pan of hot water and whisk until a meringue is formed. Remove from the heat and whisk until cool.
◆ Beat the butter until light and fluffy. Beat in the meringue a little at a time. Add the lemon rind.
◆ Split the cake into 3 layers. Spread the lemon filling between the layers. Chill.

◆ Put the chocolate and cream in a bowl over a pan of hot water. When melted, stir in the butter. Remove from heat and mix until smooth.
◆ Coat the cake with the frosting. Decorate with candied lemon slices. Allow frosting to set before serving.

Easy Chocolate Truffle Cake

SERVES 16-20

9 oz semisweet chocolate, chopped
1 cup pieces unsalted butter
¼ cup sugar
½ cup whipping cream
1 tbsp vanilla extract
6 eggs

Chocolate glaze
6 oz semisweet chocolate, chopped
¼ cup butter, cut into pieces

To decorate
whipped cream
rose petals

◆ Preheat the oven to 350°F. Grease a 9 inch, 2 inch deep round springform pan; line the bottom with waxed paper and grease the paper. Wrap the bottom of the pan in foil.
◆ Melt the chocolate, butter, and sugar with the cream, stirring until smooth; cool slightly. Stir in the vanilla extract.
◆ Beat the eggs lightly, about 1 minute. Slowly beat the chocolate into the eggs until blended.
◆ Place the pan into larger roasting pan and pour boiling water into the roasting pan, about ¾ inch up the sides of the springform pan. Bake for 25-30 minutes, until the edge of the cake is set, but the center is still soft. Remove the pan from water-bath and remove the foil. Cool on a wire rack completely; the cake will sink in the center and may be cracked.
◆ Remove the side of the pan and turn the cake onto a wire rack placed over a baking sheet to catch any drips. Remove the base and paper.
◆ In a saucepan over a low heat, melt the chocolate and butter, stirring until smooth. Pour over the cake, tilting the rack slightly to spread the glaze.
◆ With a metal spatula, carefully slide the cake onto a serving dish. If you like, pipe a whipped cream border around the edge. Dip the rose petals in lightly beaten egg white, then in fine granulated sugar. Allow to stand on waxed paper in a cool place for about 2 hours. Place in the center of the cake. Serve with softly whipped cream on the side.

RIGHT *Easy Chocolate Truffle Cake*

Blackout Cake

SERVES 12-16

2¼ cups cake flour
2 tbsp cocoa powder
1 tbsp bicarbonate of soda
½ tsp salt
4 oz semisweet chocolate, chopped
¼ cup unsalted butter, softened
1½ cups sugar
3 eggs
2 tsp vanilla extract
¼ cup buttermilk
or 1 tbsp instant coffee in
1½ cups boiling water

Chocolate ganache frosting
1¼ cups heavy cream
1 lb semisweet chocolate, chopped
¼ cup butter, cut into pieces
2 tsp vanilla extract
grated chocolate to decorate
powdered sugar for dusting

◆ Preheat the oven to 350°F. Grease and flour 9 inch round, 2 inch deep cake pans.
◆ Stir together the flour, cocoa powder and bicarbonate of soda and salt. In the top of a double boiler over a low heat, melt the chocolate; set aside.
◆ In a second bowl with an electric mixer, beat the butter with the sugar until light and creamy, about 5 minutes. Add the eggs, 1 at a time, beating well after each addition. Beat in the chocolate and vanilla extract.
◆ Add the flour mixture to the batter in 2 additions alternately with the buttermilk; beat just until blended. At low speed, slowly beat in the boiling coffee until smooth, scraping the bowl once; the batter will be thin. Pour into the prepared pans.
◆ Bake for 25-30 minutes, or until a fine skewer inserted in the centers comes out with just a few crumbs attached. Cool in the pans on a wire rack for 10 minutes. Unmold and cool completely.
◆ Meanwhile, prepare the frosting. In a medium saucepan bring the cream to the boil. Remove from the heat and immediately stir in the chocolate until melted and smooth. Beat in the butter and vanilla. Cool; refrigerate for 45-55 minutes or until the frosting is soft but spreadable.
◆ Place 1 cake layer on a plate and cover with one-third of the frosting. Place the second layer on top and frost the top and sides with the remaining frosting. Press the grated chocolate onto the sides of the cake and sprinkle on top. Dust the top with powdered sugar.

Mushroom Cake

SERVES 6

2 tbsp unsweetened cocoa powder
1 tbsp boiling water
½ cup butter or margarine
⅔ cup granulated brown sugar
2 eggs, beaten
½ cup self-rising flour

Frosting
½ cup butter or margarine
1½ cups powdered sugar
2 oz semisweet chocolate, melted
½ lb marzipan (preferably "white")
apricot jam, sieved
powdered sugar or drinking chocolate
powder

◆ Preheat the oven to 350°F. Mix together the cocoa powder and water to form a paste.
◆ Put the butter or margarine, sugar, and chocolate paste into a bowl and beat until light and fluffy.
◆ Beat in the eggs a little at a time.
◆ Fold in the flour.
◆ Spread the mixture into 1 greased and base-lined, 8 inch sandwich cake pan. Bake in the oven for about 25 minutes. Turn out and cool.
◆ To make the frosting, cream together the butter or margarine and powdered sugar. Stir in the melted chocolate and beat well. Cool.
◆ Using a piping bag fitted with a star nozzle, pipe lines of frosting from

the edge of the cake to the center, to represent the underside of a mushroom.
◆ Reserve a small piece of marzipan for the stalk. Roll the remaining marzipan out to a strip about 24 inches long and wide enough to stand just above the sides of the cake.
◆ Brush the sides of the cake with apricot jam. Press the marzipan strip round the edge of the cake. Curve the top of the marzipan over the piped ridges.
◆ Shape the reserved marzipan into a stalk and place in the center of the cake. Sift a little powdered sugar or drinking chocolate powder over the frosting on the cake.

Surprise Chocolate Ring

SERVES 8

¼ cup self-rising flour
2 tbsp unsweetened cocoa powder
¼ cup soft margarine
¼ cup sugar
3 eggs
5 tbsp cherry brandy
½ cup fruit (eg strawberries,
raspberries, pitted cherries)
¼ pt heavy cream

Frosting
5 tbsp heavy cream
6 oz semisweet chocolate, grated

To decorate
Piped chocolate butterflies
(see page 19) or
chocolate dipped fruits

◆ Preheat the oven to 350°F. Sift the flour and cocoa into a mixing bowl. Add the margarine, sugar, and eggs. Beat well together.

◆ Spoon the mixture into a greased and floured 6 cup ring mold. Bake in the oven for about 35-40 minutes. Turn out and cool.

◆ Turn the cake upside down and cut a slice about ¾ inch deep off the flat base of the ring. Lift off the slice carefully and reserve.

◆ With a teaspoon, scoop out the cake in a channel about ¾ inch deep and 1 inch wide.

◆ Sprinkle 3 tbsp of the cherry brandy over the sponge.

◆ Chop the fruit and spread in the hollow.

◆ Whisk the cream until stiff. Stir in the remaining brandy. Spread the cream over the fruit.

◆ Place the reserved slice back on the cake.

◆ Invert the cake so it is the right way up.

◆ To make the frosting, put the cream into a saucepan and bring just to the boil. Add the chocolate. Stir until the chocolate melts.

◆ Cool until the mixture is thick and smooth. Pour over the cake.

◆ Put in a cool place until set.

◆ Decorate with piped chocolate butterflies, or chocolate dipped fruit.

Chocolate Meringue Gâteau

SERVES 6

3 egg whites
pinch of cream of tartar
¼ cup fine granulated sugar
¼ cup ground filberts

Sponge
½ cup cake flour
¼ cup unsweetened cocoa powder
4 eggs, separated
½ cup sugar

Chocolate cream
8 oz semisweet chocolate
2 egg yolks
2 tbsp water
½ pt heavy cream
¼ cup sugar
red jam

To decorate
mixed chopped nuts
chocolate curls
powdered sugar

◆ Preheat the oven to 300°F. Line 2 baking sheets with waxed paper. Draw a 7 inch circle on each one.
◆ Put the egg whites and cream of tartar into a bowl and whisk until stiff.
◆ Whisk in the sugar a little at a time until the mixture is thick and glossy. Fold in the nuts.
◆ Spread or pipe the meringue in the circles marked on the paper. Bake in the oven for 1 hour. Turn off the heat and leave to dry in the closed oven for a further 30 minutes, or until crisp.
◆ Remove and cool. Carefully peel away the paper.
◆ Preheat the oven to 350°F. To make the sponge, sift together the flour and cocoa.
◆ Whisk together the egg yolks and sugar until the mixture is thick and pale.
◆ Whisk the egg whites until thick, but not stiff.
◆ Fold the flour and egg whites alternately into the egg yolk mixture.
◆ Pour into a greased and lined 7 inch cake pan. Bake for about 40 minutes. Remove and cool.

◆ To make the chocolate cream, melt the chocolate. Cool slightly. Beat together the egg yolks and water.
◆ Stir the melted chocolate into the egg yolks, mixing well. Put in a pan and cook very gently for a minute. Cool.
◆ Beat together the cream and sugar until soft peaks form. Fold into the chocolate mixture. Cover and chill.
◆ To assemble the gâteau, cut the cake into 2 layers and spread each with a little red jam.
◆ Put a meringue round on a plate and spread with a little chocolate cream. Top with a layer of sponge, spread with cream and place the second meringue round on top. Spread with cream and place the second layer of sponge on top.
◆ Spread remaining chocolate cream on the top and sides of the cake.
◆ Put chopped nuts round the side of the cake. Top with chocolate curls and sprinkle with powdered sugar.

Black Forest Gâteau

SERVES 10

½ cup light cake flour
2 tbsp cocoa powder
½ tsp baking powder
5 eggs, separated
¼ cup sugar
¼ tsp cream of tartar
¼ cup butter, melted and cooled

Cherry filling
2 cups black cherries in juice or syrup,
pitted
5 tbsp cherry-flavor liqueur
2 tbsp cornstarch, dissolved in
2 tbsp water
2 cups whipping cream
2 tbsp fine granulated sugar

To decorate
Chocolate curls (see page 18)
maraschino cherries

◆ Preheat the oven to 350°F. Grease the bottom and sides of an 8 inch springform pan. Line the bottom with waxed paper; grease the paper and flour the pan.

◆ Sift together the flour, cocoa powder and baking powder. Beat the egg yolks with ¾ cup sugar until pale and thick, about 5 minutes.
◆ Beat the egg whites and cream of tartar until stiff peaks form. Sprinkle in the remaining sugar and beat until stiff and glossy.
◆ Stir 1 spoonful of egg whites into the yolk mixture to lighten. Fold in the flour and cocoa mixture and the remaining egg whites alternately just until blended. Pour the melted butter over and fold in just until blended. Spoon into the pan, spreading evenly.
◆ Bake for 30-35 minutes, until a fine skewer inserted in the center comes out clean. Cool on a wire rack for 10 minutes. Remove from the pan and cool completely.
◆ Meanwhile, prepare the filling. Drain the cherries, reserving the juice. Mix 3 tbsp cherry juice with 3 tbsp cherry-flavor liqueur; set aside. In a saucepan, stir together the remaining cherry juice and cornstarch mixture. Bring to the boil, then simmer for 2-3 minutes, until thickened. Stir in the cherries and set aside to cool.

◆ Whip the cream, sugar and remaining cherry-flavor liqueur until soft peaks form. Reserve about ½ cup cream for decoration.
◆ With a serrated knife, cut the cake horizontally into 3 layers. Place the bottom layer on a plate. Sprinkle over one-third of the cherry juice syrup and spread with about 1½ cups whipped cream. Spoon half the cherry mixture evenly over the cream and cover with a second cake layer. Sprinkle one-third of the cherry juice syrup over and another 1½ cups whipped cream. Spoon the remaining cherry mixture over. Sprinkle the cut side of the third cake layer with the remaining cherry juice syrup and place cut side down over the cherry layer. Frost the top and sides of the cake with the remaining whipped cream.
◆ Press chocolate curls onto the sides of the cake. Spoon the reserved cream into a small piping bag fitted with a medium star nozzle and pipe 10 rosettes evenly around the cake. Top each with a maraschino cherry. Refrigerate.

Classic Devil's Food Cake

SERVES 10-12

2 oz semisweet chocolate, chopped
½ cup cocoa powder
2¼ cups cake flour
2 tsp bicarbonate of soda
½ tsp salt
½ cup unsalted butter, softened
2½ cups granulated brown sugar
1 tbsp vanilla extract
3 eggs
¼ cup sour cream
1 tsp vinegar
1 cup boiling water

Chocolate ganache frosting
3 cups whipping cream
1½ lb semisweet chocolate, chopped
1 tbsp vanilla extract

RIGHT *Classic Devil's Food Cake*

◆ Preheat the oven to 375°F. Butter 2 9 inch round cake pans, 1½ inches deep. Line the bottoms with waxed paper; butter the paper and flour the pans.
◆ In the top of a double boiler over a low heat, melt the chocolate, stirring frequently until smooth. Set aside. Sift together the cocoa powder, flour, bicarbonate of soda, and salt.
◆ With an electric mixer, cream the butter, brown sugar and vanilla extract until light and creamy, about 5 minutes, scraping the side of the bowl occasionally. Add the eggs, 1 at a time, beating well after each addition.
◆ Add the flour mixture alternately with the sour cream in 3 batches, beating until well blended. Stir in the vinegar and slowly beat in the boiling water; the batter will be thin. Pour into the pans.
◆ Bake for 20-25 minutes, until a fine skewer inserted in the center comes out with just a few crumbs attached. Cool the cakes in pans on a wire rack.

Remove the cakes from the pans. Remove from the paper and cool on a wire rack while preparing the frosting.
◆ In a saucepan over a medium heat, bring the cream to the boil. Remove from the heat and stir in the chocolate all at once until melted and smooth. Cool slightly. Pour into a large bowl and refrigerate for 1 hour, stirring twice, until the frosting is spreadable.
◆ With a serrated knife, slice each cake layer horizontally into 2 layers. Place 1 cake layer cut-side up on a cake plate and spread with one-sixth of the frosting. Place a second layer on top and cover with another sixth of the frosting. Place a third layer on top and cover with another sixth of the frosting, then cover with the fourth cake layer top-side (rounded) up. Frost the top and sides of the cake with the remaining sugar. Serve at room temperature.

Refrigerator Cookie Cake

SERVES 6

8 oz milk chocolate
½ cup butter
¼ cup corn syrup
¼ cup raisins, soaked overnight in a little rum
½ cup Brazil nuts, roughly chopped
¼ cup maraschino cherries, roughly chopped
1 cup wholewheat cookies, crushed

To decorate
maraschino cherries
whole Brazil nuts

◆ Put the chocolate, butter, and corn syrup into a bowl over a pan of hot water.
◆ When the chocolate has melted, stir in the raisins, nuts, and cherries.
◆ Add the cookies and mix well together.
◆ Line a 1 lb loaf pan with waxed paper. Press the mixture into the pan.
◆ Chill for at least 4 hours, preferably overnight.
◆ Turn out and decorate with maraschino cherries and Brazil nuts.

Chocolate-Chestnut Roulade

SERVES 12

Roulade sponge
6 oz semisweet chocolate, chopped
½ cup strong coffee
6 eggs, separated
9 tbsp fine granulated sugar
½ tsp cream of tartar
2 tsp vanilla extract
cocoa powder for dusting

Chestnut cream filling
2 cups heavy cream
3 tbsp coffee-flavor liqueur
or 2 tsp vanilla extract
2 cups canned sweetened chestnut
purée

To decorate
powdered sugar
candied chestnuts

◆ Preheat the oven to 350°F. Grease the base and sides of a 15½ x 10½ x 1 inch jelly roll pan. Line the base with waxed paper, allowing 1 inch to overhang; grease and flour the paper.
◆ Melt the chocolate with the coffee, stirring frequently until smooth. Set aside.
◆ Beat the egg yolks with half the sugar until pale and thick, about 5 minutes. Slowly beat in the chocolate just until blended.
◆ In another large bowl, with an electric mixer, beat the egg whites and cream of tartar until stiff peaks form. Gradually sprinkle the sugar over the egg whites in 2 batches and continue beating until the egg whites are stiff and glossy; beat in the vanilla extract.
◆ Stir 1 spoonful of egg whites into the chocolate mixture to lighten, then fold in the remaining egg whites. Spoon into the prepared pan, spreading evenly.
◆ Bake for 12-15 minutes, or until the cake springs back when touched with a fingertip.

◆ Meanwhile, dust a dish towel with cocoa powder. When the cake is done, turn out onto the towel immediately and remove the paper. Starting at a narrow end, roll the cake and towel together jelly-roll fashion. Cool completely.
◆ With an electric mixer, whip the cream and coffee-flavor liqueur or vanilla extract until soft peaks form. Beat 1 spoonful of cream into the chestnut purée to lighten, then fold in the remaining cream.
◆ Unroll the cake and trim the edges. Spread the chestnut cream mixture to within 1 inch of the edge of the cake. Using the towel to lift the cake, roll the cake.
◆ Place the roulade seam-side down on a serving plate. Decorate the roulade with bands of sifted powdered sugar and candied chestnuts.

Bûche de Noël

SERVES 6-8

4 eggs, separated
½ cup sugar
1 cup cake flour

Butter cream
¼ cup sugar
6 tbsp water
4 egg yolks
¼ cup unsalted butter
3 oz semisweet chocolate, melted
1-2 tsp dark rum

To decorate
Meringue Mushrooms (see page 134)
marzipan holly leaves and berries

◆ Preheat the oven to 450°F. Grease and line a 9 x 13 inch jelly roll pan.
◆ Put the egg yolks and sugar into a mixing bowl and whisk until the mixture falls in a thick trail.

◆ Whisk the egg whites until stiff.
◆ Fold the egg whites and flour alternately into the egg yolk mixture. Pour into the pan and bake in the oven for about 10 minutes until golden brown.
◆ Put a sheet of waxed paper on top of a dampened dish towel and sprinkle with fine granulated sugar. Turn the sponge out onto the sugared paper.
◆ Peel off the lining paper and quickly trim the edges of the sponge. Make a shallow groove across one short side of the cake 1 inch from the edge.
◆ Fold the sponge over at the groove. Using the towel as support, roll up the sponge with the waxed paper inside. Cover with the damp cloth until cold.
◆ To make the butter cream, put the sugar and water into a small pan. Dissolve the sugar and then bring to the boil and boil to the "thread" stage (225°F).

◆ Whisk the egg yolks in a bowl until thick and creamy. Slowly pour the hot syrup onto the egg yolks in a steady stream, beating constantly until the mixture is light and fluffy.
◆ Beat the butter until soft. Add the egg mixture a little at a time until the mixture is firm and shiny. Stir in the chocolate and rum.
◆ Carefully unroll the sponge and remove the waxed paper. Spread a little butter cream over the sponge and roll up again.
◆ Put the cake onto a serving dish. Spoon the remaining butter cream into a piping bag fitted with a star nozzle. Pipe lines lengthways down the cake. Add an occasional swirl to represent a "knot" on a log.
◆ Decorate with Meringue Mushrooms and marzipan holly leaves and berries.

$\mathcal{P}$IES *and* $\mathcal{P}$ASTRIES

Chocolate Chiffon Pie

SERVES 6-8

6 oz pie dough
½ cup milk
¼ cup sugar
4 oz semisweet chocolate, chopped
2 small eggs, separated
2 tsp powdered gelatin
2 tbsp water
¼ pt heavy cream

To decorate
whipped cream
chocolate curls (see page 18)

◆ Preheat the oven to 375°F. Roll out the dough and use to line an 8 inch pie plate. Bake "blind" (lined with waxed paper and baking beans) in the oven for 20-25 minutes. Remove the waxed paper and baking beans and return to the oven for a further 5-10 minutes until crisp and lightly browned. Leave to cool.
◆ Put the milk, 1 tbsp sugar and chocolate into a saucepan and melt over a gentle heat. Stir continuously. Cool slightly.
◆ Whisk the egg yolks into the chocolate mixture.

◆ Dissolve the gelatin in the water and stir into the chocolate. Leave until the mixture is beginning to thicken and set.
◆ Whisk the egg whites until stiff. Whisk in the remaining sugar.
◆ Whisk the cream until it stands in soft peaks.
◆ Fold the egg whites and cream thoroughly into the chocolate mixture. Pour into the pie shell. Chill until set.
◆ To serve, pipe whipped cream over the top and pile chocolate curls in the center.

Chocolate and Pecan Pie

SERVES 8-10

1¼ cups all-purpose flour
1 tbsp fine granulated sugar
½ tsp salt
½ cup small pieces butter
½ cup ice water

Filling
3 oz semisweet chocolate, chopped
2 tbsp butter, cut into pieces
3 eggs
¼ cup light brown sugar
6 tbsp corn syrup
1 tbsp vanilla extract
1 cup pecan halves
3 oz milk or semisweet chocolate chips
(optional)

◆ Prepare the pie dough. In a food processor fitted with a metal blade, process the flour, sugar, and salt to blend. Add the butter and process for 15-20 seconds, until the mixture resembles coarse crumbs. With the machine running, add ice water through the feeder tube, just until the dough begins to stick together; do not allow the dough to form a ball or the pastry will be tough.

◆ Turn the dough onto a floured work surface, shape into a flat disc and wrap tightly in plastic wrap. Refrigerate for 1 hour.
◆ Lightly butter a 9 inch pie plate, 1½ inches deep. Soften the dough for 10-15 minutes at room temperature. On a well-floured surface, roll out the dough into a 12 inch circle about ¼ inch thick. Roll the dough loosely around the rolling pin and unroll over the pie plate; ease the dough into the plate.
◆ With kitchen scissors, trim the dough, leaving about a ¼ inch overhang; flatten to the rim of the pie plate, pressing slightly towards the center of the plate. With a small knife, cut out hearts or other shapes from the dough trimmings. Brush the dough edge with water and press the dough shapes to the edge. Prick the bottom of dough with a fork. Refrigerate for 30 minutes.
◆ Preheat the oven to 400°F. Line the pie shell with foil or waxed paper and fill with dry beans or rice. Bake for 5 minutes, then lift out foil or paper with the beans and bake for 5 minutes longer. Remove to a wire rack to cool slightly. Lower the oven

temperature to 375°F.
◆ In a saucepan over a low heat, melt the chocolate and butter, stirring until smooth. Set aside.
◆ In a bowl, beat together the eggs, sugar, corn syrup and vanilla extract. Slowly beat in the melted chocolate. Sprinkle the pecan halves and chocolate chips (if using) over the bottom of the pastry. Place the pie plate on a baking sheet and carefully pour in the chocolate mixture.
◆ Bake for 35-40 minutes, until the chocolate mixture is set; the top may crack slightly. If the pastry edges begin to overbrown, cover with strips of foil. Transfer to a wire rack to cool. Serve warm with softly whipped cream.

Chocolate Cream Pie

SERVES 8

8 oz semisweet chocolate wholewheat
cookies
¼ cup butter, melted
6 oz semisweet chocolate, chopped
1 cup whipping cream
⅓ cup cornstarch
1 tbsp all-purpose flour
¼ cup fine granulated sugar
a scant 3 cups milk
5 egg yolks
3 tbsp butter, softened

Light whipped cream
1½ cups heavy cream
2 egg whites
¼ tsp cream of tartar
¼ cup sugar
2 tsp vanilla extract
cocoa powder for dusting

◆ Preheat the oven to 350°F. Lightly butter a 9 inch, 1½ inch deep pie pan or fluted pie plate.
◆ In a food processor, process the chocolate cookies until fine crumbs form. Pour in the melted butter and process just until blended. Pat onto the bottom and sides of the pie plate.

◆ Bake for 5-7 minutes, just until set. Transfer to a wire rack to cool completely.
◆ In a saucepan over low heat, melt the chocolate with the whipping cream, stirring until smooth. Set aside.
◆ In another saucepan, combine the cornstarch, flour, and sugar. Gradually stir in the milk and cook over medium heat until thickened and bubbling.
◆ In a bowl, beat the egg yolks lightly. Slowly pour 1 cup hot milk into the yolks, stirring constantly. Return the egg-yolk mixture to the pan and bring to a gentle boil, stirring constantly. Cook for 1 minute longer. Stir in the butter and melted chocolate until well blended. Pour into the prepared shell and place a piece of plastic wrap directly against the surface of the filling to prevent a skin forming. Cool, then refrigerate until completely chilled.
◆ With an electric mixer, whip the cream until soft peaks form. In another bowl, with an electric mixer and clean blades, beat the egg whites and cream of tartar until stiff peaks form. Gradually sprinkle the sugar

over in 2 batches, beating well after each addition, until the whites are stiff and glossy. Beat in the vanilla extract.
◆ Fold 1 spoonful of egg white into the cream to lighten, then fold the remaining egg whites into the cream. Peel the plastic wrap from the chilled custard; spread the cream onto the custard in a swirling pattern. Dust the cream lightly with cocoa powder.

White Chocolate Mousse and Strawberry Tart

SERVES 10-12

½ cup butter, softened
¼ cup fine granulated sugar
½ tsp salt
3 egg yolks
1 tsp vanilla extract
1¼ cups all-purpose flour

Strawberry filling
2 lb fresh, ripe strawberries
2 tbsp cherry-flavor liqueur

White chocolate mousse filling
9 oz white chocolate, chopped
3 tbsp cherry-flavor liqueur
2 tbsp water
1½ cups heavy cream
2 egg whites (optional)
¼ tsp cream of tartar (optional)

To decorate
1 oz white chocolate, melted, or white
chocolate curls (see page 18)
2 tbsp seedless strawberry jam, melted
and cooled

SWEET SUCCESS

Be sure to allow the melted white chocolate to cool to below body temperature so it does not deflate the whipped cream. A small dab should feel cool when touched to your upper lip, about 85°F. The pie shell can be made ahead, but the shell should be filled and assembled the same day it is to be served to prevent the berries from bleeding into the mousse mixture and the mousse from becoming too firm when refrigerated.

◆ Prepare the pastry. In a bowl, with a hand-held electric mixer, beat the butter with the sugar and salt until creamy, about 2 minutes. Add the egg yolks and vanilla extract and beat until smooth. Add half the flour to the butter and egg mixture, then stir in the remaining flour by hand until well blended.

◆ Place a piece of plastic wrap on a work surface. Scrape the dough onto the plastic wrap. Use the plastic wrap to help shape the dough into a flat disc and wrap tightly. Refrigerate for 1 hour.

◆ Lightly butter a 10 inch pie plate with a removable base. Soften the dough for 10 minutes at room temperature. On a well-floured surface, roll out the dough to an 11½-12 inch circle about ⅛ inch thick. Roll the dough loosely around the rolling pin and unroll over the pie plate. Ease the dough into the plate, patching if necessary.

◆ With floured fingers, press the overhang down slightly toward the center, making the top edge thicker. Roll the rolling pin over the plate edge to cut off the excess dough. Press the thicker top edge against the side of the plate to form a rim about ¼ inch higher than the plate. Using your thumb and forefinger, crimp the edge. Prick the bottom of the dough with a fork. Refrigerate for 1 hour.

◆ Preheat the oven to 375°F. Line the shell with foil or waxed paper; fill with dry beans or rice. Bake for 10 minutes; lift out the foil or paper with the beans and bake for 5-7 minutes longer until set and golden. Remove to a wire rack to cool completely.

◆ Prepare the strawberry filling. Cut the strawberries in half lengthways. In a bowl, mash about 1½ cups strawberry halves with the cherry-

flavor liqueur. Set the remaining berries and the mashed berries aside.

◆ Prepare the mousse. In a saucepan over a low heat, melt the white chocolate with the cherry-flavor liqueur, water and ½ cup cream, stirring until smooth. Set aside to cool.

◆ With an electric mixer, beat the remaining cream until soft peaks form. Stir 1 spoonful of cream into the chocolate mixture to lighten, then fold in the remaining cream. If you like, beat the egg whites with the cream of tartar until stiff peaks form then fold them into the chocolate cream mixture to make a lighter, softer mousse.

◆ Pour about one-third of the mousse mixture into the cooled shell. Spread the mashed berries evenly over the mousse, then cover with the remaining mousse mixture.

◆ To serve, arrange the sliced strawberries cut side up in concentric circles around the tart to cover the mousse. Remove the side of the pan and slide the tart onto a serving platter. Spoon the melted white chocolate into a paper cone and drizzle the white chocolate over the tart; alternatively, decorate the center with white chocolate curls, or glaze with seedless strawberry jam.

Rich Chocolate Meringue Pie

SERVES 6

8 oz wholewheat cookies
½ cup butter

Filling
2 tbsp sugar
¼ cup all-purpose flour
2 level tsp cornstarch
2 egg yolks
1¼ cups milk
2 tbsp butter
4 oz semisweet chocolate, finely
chopped
2 tsp rum (optional)

Topping
2 egg whites
½ cup fine granulated sugar
ground cinnamon

◆ Preheat the oven to 400°F. Crush the cookies until they resemble fine breadcrumbs.
◆ Melt the butter and stir into the crumbs. Press the crumbs over the base and sides of an 8 inch ovenproof pie plate.
◆ Blend together the sugar, flour, cornstarch, egg yolks, and a little of the milk. Heat the remaining milk.
◆ Stir the hot milk onto the flour mixture and whisk well. Return the mixture to the pan. Heat gently, stirring until the mixture thickens.
◆ Stir in the butter, chocolate, and rum if used. Stir until smooth. Pour into the pie shell. Chill.
◆ About 30 minutes before serving, make the meringue topping. Whisk the egg whites until stiff.

◆ Whisk in half the sugar a teaspoonful at a time. Add the remaining sugar and whisk well.
◆ Spread the meringue over the chocolate flan. Swirl decoratively with a teaspoon.
◆ Bake in the oven for 3-5 minutes, until the meringue is golden brown.
◆ Sprinkle with a little ground cinnamon.

Mississippi Mud Pie

SERVES 8

6 oz wholewheat cookies
large knob of butter, melted
4 oz semisweet chocolate, melted
5 cups coffee ice cream
5 cups chocolate ice cream
2 tbsp Tia Maria
2 tbsp brandy

To decorate
whipped cream
grated chocolate

◆ Crush the cookies in a food processor or in a plastic food bag with a rolling pin.

◆ Stir in the butter and chocolate and mix well together.

◆ Press the crumbs firmly and evenly over the bottom and sides of a greased 9 inch pie plate. Chill.

◆ Allow the ice creams to soften slightly. Put in a bowl and add the Tia Maria and brandy. Blend well together.

◆ Spoon the ice cream into the chocolate case and put in the freezer until solid.

◆ Remove the pie from the freezer about 15 minutes before serving. Decorate with whipped cream and grated chocolate.

Black-Bottom Lemon Tartlets

MAKES 12

1½ cups all-purpose flour
2 tbsp powdered sugar
½ tsp salt
3 cups unsalted butter, cut into pieces
and at room temperature
1 egg yolk
½ tsp vanilla extract
2-3 tbsp cold water

Lemon custard sauce
1 lemon
1½ cups milk
6 egg yolks
⅓ cup sugar

Lemon cheese filling
2 lemons
3 cups unsalted butter,
cut into pieces
1 cup sugar
3 eggs

Chocolate filling
¼ cup cream
6 oz semisweet chocolate, chopped
2 tbsp unsalted butter,
cut into pieces

To decorate
Chocolate triangles (see page 18)
1 oz semisweet chocolate, melted

SWEET SUCCESS

Pastry and tartlets can be prepared
a day ahead. These tartlets are best
filled just a few hours before serving
so fillings are still soft.
An easy way to blind bake tartlets
is to use cupcake papers. One
small paper just covers the bottom
and sides of a 3 inch tartlet mold.

◆ First prepare the custard sauce. With a swivel-bladed vegetable peeler, remove strips of rind from the lemon. Place in a medium saucepan over a medium heat with the milk and bring to the boil. Remove from the heat and leave for 5 minutes to infuse. Reheat the milk gently.

◆ Beat the egg yolks and sugar until pale and thick, 2-3 minutes. Pour about 1 cup hot milk over, beating vigorously. Return the egg yolk mixture to the pan and cook gently over a low heat until the mixture thickens; do not let it boil or it will curdle. Strain into a chilled bowl. Squeeze 2 tbsp juice from the lemon and stir into the sauce. Cool, stirring occasionally. Refrigerate until ready to use.

◆ Prepare the lemon cheese filling. Grate the rind and squeeze the juice of the lemons into the top of a double boiler. Add the butter and sugar and stir over medium heat until the butter is melted and sugar dissolved. Lower the heat. In a bowl, lightly beat the eggs, then string into the butter mixture. Cook over a low heat, stirring until the mixture thickens, about 15 minutes. Pour (or strain if you do not want the lemon rind) into a bowl. Cool, stirring occasionally. Refrigerate to thicken.

◆ Prepare the pastry. Place the flour, sugar, and salt into a food processor fitted with a metal blade. Process to blend. Add the butter and process for 15-20 seconds, until the mixture resembles coarse crumbs. In a bowl, beat the egg yolk with the vanilla extract and water. With the food processor running, pour the egg yolk mixture through the feed tube just until the dough begins to stick together; do not allow the dough to form a ball or the pastry will be tough. If the dough appears too dry add 1-2 tbsp more cold water.

◆ Place a piece of plastic wrap on a work surface. Turn the dough out onto the plastic wrap. Use the plastic wrap to help shape the dough into a flat disc. Wrap tightly and refrigerate for at least 30 minutes.

◆ Lightly butter 12 3 inch pie plates (if possible, with removable bases). On a lightly floured surface, roll out the dough to an oblong shape slightly more than ⅛ inch thick. Using a 4 inch fluted cutter, cut out 12 circles and press each one onto the bottom and sides of the pie plates. Prick the bottom of the dough with a fork. Place the pie plates on a large baking sheet and refrigerate for 30 minutes.

◆ Preheat the oven to 375°F. Cut out 12 5 inch circles of foil and line each pie plate; fill with dry beans or rice. Bake for 5-8 minutes; remove the foil with the beans and bake for 5 minutes longer, until golden. Transfer the tartlets to a wire rack to cool.

◆ Prepare the chocolate filling. In a saucepan over a medium heat, bring the cream to the boil. Remove from the heat and stir in the chocolate until melted and smooth. Beat in the butter and leave to cool slightly.

◆ Spoon an equal amount of chocolate filling into each tartlet. Refrigerate for 10 minutes.

◆ Onto each chocolate-filled tartlet, spoon a layer of lemon cheese. Set aside, but do not refrigerate or the chocolate layer will be too firm.

◆ Spoon a little custard onto dessert plates. Remove the tartlets from the pie plates and place in the center of the plates. Decorate each tartlet with a chocolate triangle. If you like, spoon melted chocolate into a paper cone, and make drops or chocolate circles. Draw a toothpick or skewer through the circles to marble into the custard or make a heart motif.

Mocha-Fudge Pie with Coffee Custard Cream

SERVES 10

4 oz semisweet chocolate, chopped
½ cup butter, cut into pieces
4 eggs
1 tbsp corn syrup
½ cup sugar
1 tbsp instant coffee powder, dissolved
in 2-3 tbsp hot water
1 tsp ground cinnamon
a scant 4 tbsp milk

Coffee custard cream
3½ cups milk
1 tbsp instant coffee powder, dissolved
in 1-2 tbsp hot water
¾ cup sugar
6 egg yolks
2 tsp cornstarch
2 tbsp coffee-flavor liqueur

To decorate
whipped cream
chocolate-coated coffee beans

◆ Preheat the oven to 350°F. Lightly grease a 9 inch pie plate, 1½ inches deep.
◆ In a saucepan over a low heat, melt the chocolate and butter, stirring until smooth. Set aside.
◆ In a bowl, beat the eggs lightly. Blend in the corn syrup, sugar, dissolved coffee powder, cinnamon, and milk. Stir in the chocolate mixture until well blended. Place the pie plate on a baking sheet. Pour the chocolate mixture into the pie plate.
◆ Bake for 20-25 minutes, or until the edge is set but the center is still almost liquid. Transfer to a wire rack to cool completely; the top may crack slightly.
◆ Prepare the custard. In a saucepan over medium heat, bring the milk and dissolved coffee powder to the boil. In a bowl, beat the sugar and egg yolks until pale and thick, 3-5 minutes. Stir in the cornstarch just until blended.

◆ Slowly pour about 1 cup hot milk into the yolks, stirring constantly. Return the yolk mixture to the pan and cook over a low heat, stirring constantly, until the sauce thickens, 5-8 minutes; do not allow the sauce to boil or it will curdle. Strain into a chilled bowl and stir until slightly cool. Stir in the coffee-flavor liqueur and cool completely. Refrigerate until ready to serve.
◆ To serve, place a spoonful of custard on a dessert plate and place a slice of pie on the pool of custard. If you like, garnish with softly whipped cream and chocolate-coated coffee beans.

White Chocolate and Banana Cream Tart

SERVES 8

1½ cups all-purpose flour
¼ cup shredded sweetened coconut
½ cup butter, softened
3 tbsp fine granulated sugar
2 egg yolks
½ tsp almond extract

White chocolate custard
5 oz good-quality white chocolate, chopped
½ cup heavy cream
⅓ cup cornstarch
1 tbsp all-purpose flour
⅓ cup sugar
2 cups milk
5 egg yolks
2¼ cups whipping cream
½ tsp almond extract
3 very ripe bananas
a scant ½ cup chopped almonds, toasted

◆ Prepare the pastry. With an electric mixer at low speed, combine the flour, coconut, butter, sugar, egg yolks, and almond extract until blended.
◆ Press the dough onto the bottom and sides of a lightly buttered pie plate with removable base. Prick the dough with a fork. Refrigerate for 30 minutes.
◆ Preheat the oven to 350°F. Line the shell with foil or waxed paper; fill with dry beans or rice. Bake for 10 minutes. Lift out the foil or paper with the beans and bake for 5-7 minutes longer, until golden. Cool on a wire rack.
◆ Prepare the custard. Melt the white chocolate with the cream, stirring until smooth. Set aside.
◆ Combine the cornstarch, flour, and sugar. Stir in the milk and cook until thickened and bubbling.

◆ Beat the egg yolks lightly. Slowly pour about 1 cup hot milk into the yolks, stirring constantly. Return the egg yolk mixture to the pan and bring to a gentle boil, stirring constantly. Cook for 1-2 minutes longer. Stir in the melted chocolate until well blended. Cool to room temperature, stirring frequently to prevent a skin from forming.
◆ With an electric mixer, beat the whipping cream with the almond extract until soft peaks form. Fold about ½ cup whipped cream into the white chocolate custard.
◆ Slice the bananas and line the bottom of the pie shell with the slices. Pour the white chocolate custard over and spread evenly. Remove the side of the pie plate and slide onto a plate.
◆ Pipe the remaining cream in a scroll pattern in parallel rows, ½ inch apart. Sprinkle the chopped toasted almonds between the rows.

Chocolate and Pine Nut Tart

SERVES 7-8

Sweet French tart pastry
1½ cups all-purpose flour
¼ cup fine granulated sugar
¼ tsp salt
½ cup butter, cut into small pieces
3 egg yolks, lightly beaten
1-2 tbsp ice water

Filling
2 eggs
⅓ cup sugar
rind of 1 orange, grated
1 tbsp orange-flavor liqueur
1 cup whipping cream
4 oz semisweet chocolate, chopped
½ cup pine nuts, toasted

Glaze
1 orange
½ cup water
¼ cup sugar
1 tbsp cold water

◆ Prepare the pastry. In a food processor fitted with a metal blade, process the flour, sugar, and salt to blend. Add the butter and process for 15-20 seconds, until the mixture resembles coarse crumbs. Add the egg yolks and using pulse action, process just until the dough begins to stick together; do not allow the dough to form a ball or the pastry will be tough. If the dough appears dry, add 1-2 tbsp ice water, little by little, just until the dough holds together.

◆ Turn the dough onto a lightly floured work surface and using a pastry scraper to scrape the dough, knead gently until well blended. Shape the dough into a flat disc and wrap tightly in plastic wrap. Refrigerate for 4-5 hours.

◆ Lightly butter a 9 inch, 1½ inch deep pie plate with a removable base. Soften the dough for 5-10 minutes at room temperature. On a well-floured surface, roll out the dough into an 11 inch circle about ¼ inch thick. Roll the dough loosely around the rolling pin and unroll over the pie plate; ease the dough into the plate.

◆ With floured fingers, press the overhang down slightly toward the center, making the top edge thicker, then roll the rolling pin over the plate edge to cut off the excess dough. Press the thicker top edge against the side of the plate to form a rim about ¼ inch higher than the plate. Using thumb and forefinger, crimp the edge. Prick the bottom of the dough with a fork. Refrigerate for 1 hour.

◆ Preheat the oven to 400°F. Line the shell with foil or waxed paper and fill with dry beans or rice. Bake for 5 minutes, lift out the foil or paper with the beans and bake for 5 minutes longer, just until set. Remove to a wire rack to cool slightly. Lower the oven temperature to 375°F.

◆ In a bowl, beat together the eggs, sugar, orange rind, and orange-flavor liqueur. Blend in the cream.

◆ Sprinkle chopped chocolate evenly over the bottom of the shell, then sprinkle pine nuts over. Place the plate on a baking sheet and gently pour the egg-and-cream mixture into the shell.

◆ Bake for 30-35 minutes, until the pastry is golden and the egg mixture is set. Transfer to a wire rack to cool for 10 minutes.

◆ Prepare the glaze. With a swivel-bladed vegetable peeler, remove thin strips of orange rind and cut into julienne strips. In a saucepan over high heat, bring the orange strips, water, and sugar to the boil. Boil for 5-8 minutes, until the syrup is thickened; stir in the cold water.

◆ With a pastry brush, glaze the tart with sugar syrup and arrange the julienne orange strips over the top. Remove the side of the pie plate and slide the tart onto a plate. Serve the tart warm.

Chocolate Syrup Tart

SERVES 8

2 cups all-purpose flour
3 tbsp powdered sugar
1 cup butter
a little water
4 oz semisweet chocolate
3 eggs
a scant 4 tbsp corn syrup
1 cup sugar
1 tsp vanilla extract
vanilla ice cream

◆ Preheat the oven to 350°F. Sift the flour and powdered sugar into a bowl. Rub in ⅔ cup butter until the mixture resembles fine crumbs.
◆ Add enough water to mix to a stiff dough.
◆ Roll out the pastry and use to line a 9 inch pie plate.
◆ Put the remaining butter and the chocolate into a saucepan. Stir over gentle heat until melted and blended.
◆ Beat the eggs, syrup, sugar, and vanilla extract together. Stir in the chocolate mixture.

◆ Pour the filling into the pie shell. Bake in the oven for about 40 minutes, until the top is crunchy and the filling set. (The filling should be soft inside.)
◆ Serve warm with scoops of vanilla ice cream.

Chocolate Truffle Tart

SERVES 10

1 cup all-purpose flour
3 tbsp cocoa powder
¼ cup fine granulated sugar
½ tsp salt
½ cup well-chilled butter, cut into
pieces
1 egg yolk
1-2 tbsp ice water

Truffle filling
1¼ cups heavy cream
12 oz semisweet chocolate, chopped
3 tbsp butter, cut into pieces
1-2 tbsp orange-flavor liqueur or
brandy (optional)
1 oz good-quality white chocolate,
melted

◆ First prepare the pastry. Sift the flour and cocoa powder into a bowl. In a food processor fitted with a metal blade, process the flour mixture, sugar, and salt to blend. Add the butter and process for 15-20 seconds, until the mixture resembles coarse crumbs.

◆ In another bowl, lightly beat the egg yolk with the ice water. Add to the flour mixture and, using pulse action, process just until the dough begins to stick together; do not allow the dough to form into a ball or the pastry will be tough. The dough should be soft and creamy and may be difficult to handle. Place a piece of plastic wrap on a work surface. Turn out the dough onto the plastic wrap. Use the plastic wrap to help shape the dough into a flat disc and wrap tightly. Refrigerate for 1-2 hours.

◆ Lightly grease a 9 inch pie plate, 1½ inches deep, with a removable base. Soften the dough for 5-10 minutes at room temperature. Roll out the dough between 2 sheets of waxed paper or plastic wrap to an 11 inch circle about ¼ inch thick. Peel off the top sheet of waxed paper or plastic wrap and invert the dough into the plate. Remove the bottom layer of paper or plastic wrap. Press the dough onto the bottom and sides of the plate. Prick the bottom of the dough with a fork. Refrigerate for 1 hour.

◆ Preheat the oven to 375°F. Line the shell with foil or waxed paper; fill with dried beans or rice. Bake 5-7 minutes; lift out foil or paper with the beans and bake for 5-7 minutes longer, just until set. The base of the pastry may look slightly underdone, but it will dry out. Transfer to a wire rack to cool completely.

◆ Prepare the filling. In a saucepan over a medium heat, bring the cream to the boil. Remove the pan from the heat and stir in the chocolate until melted and smooth. Stir in the butter and liqueur.

◆ Strain into the shell, tilting slightly to even the surface, but do not touch the surface.

◆ Spoon the melted white chocolate into a paper cone and cut the tip about ¼ inch in diameter. Drizzle white chocolate over the surface of the dark chocolate in an abstract design. Refrigerate for 2-3 hours, until set. To serve, leave the tart to soften slightly at room temperature, about 30 minutes.

BREADS

Chocolate Ring Doughnuts

Makes About 12

2 cups all-purpose flour
½ tsp bicarbonate of soda
1 tsp cream of tartar
2 tbsp butter
⅓ cup granulated brown sugar
2 oz semisweet chocolate
1 tsp vanilla extract
1 egg, beaten
milk
oil for deep frying
fine granulated sugar mixed with
ground cinnamon

Frosting
4 oz semisweet chocolate
¼ cup + 2 tsp milk and water mixed
1½ cups powdered sugar, sifted

◆ Sift the flour, bicarbonate of soda, and cream of tartar into a bowl.
◆ Blend in the butter and stir in the sugar.
◆ Melt the chocolate and vanilla extract together.
◆ Pour the beaten egg and chocolate into the dry ingredients and mix to a stiff dough, adding a little milk if necessary.
◆ Knead very lightly and roll out until about ½ inch thick.
◆ Using a floured ring cutter (or a large and small round pastry cutter) stamp out the doughnuts. Reserve the centers.
◆ Heat the oil to 360°F and fry the doughnuts a few at a time until golden brown. Drain and cool.

◆ Cook the doughnut centers (called doughnut "holes"). Drain. While still warm, toss in fine granulated sugar which has cinnamon added to it. Serve the doughnut holes warm.
◆ To make the frosting, melt the chocolate and liquid together. Add the powdered sugar and beat well.
◆ Spread the frosting over the cooled doughnut rings.

Chocolate Croissants

MAKES ABOUT 12

4 cups all-purpose flour
1 tsp salt
2 tbsp shortening
1 oz fresh yeast
1 cup tepid water
1 egg, beaten
¼ cup butter
8 oz chocolate chips
2 tsp water
1 tsp sugar

◆ Sift together the flour and salt. Blend in the shortening.
◆ Blend the yeast with the water. Add the yeast liquid and egg to the flour and mix to a soft dough.
◆ Knead lightly on a floured surface for 10-15 minutes until smooth. Roll out to a strip measuring 20 x 8 inches.
◆ Soften the butter and divide into 3. Dot 1 portion of the butter over two-thirds of the dough. Fold the dough in 3, folding up the unbuttered portion first. Seal the edge with a rolling pin. Wrap in plastic wrap and chill.
◆ Repeat twice more, using the other 2 portions of butter. Wrap in plastic wrap and chill.
◆ Roll out and fold 3 more times. Chill for at least 1 hour.

◆ Roll out to a rectangle measuring 22 x 12 inches. Trim the edges and cut in half lengthways. Cut each strip into triangles.
◆ At the base of each triangle put a little pile of chocolate chips.
◆ Beat together the egg, water and sugar. Brush over the edges of each croissant.
◆ Roll up each croissant loosely, starting at the base and finishing with the tip underneath.
◆ Put onto a baking sheet and shape.
◆ Cover with greased plastic wrap and leave to rise for 20-30 minutes. Brush with egg glaze.
◆ Preheat the oven to 425˚F. Bake the croissants in the oven for about 20 minutes. Cool on a wire rack. Serve warm.

Chocolate Muffins

MAKES 12

2 cups all-purpose flour
3 tbsp unsweetened cocoa powder
¼ cup sugar
1 tsp baking powder
a pinch of salt
¼ cup raisins
1 egg, beaten
1 cup milk
¼ cup corn oil

◆ Preheat the oven to 400°F. Sift the flour and cocoa powder into a bowl. Stir in the sugar, baking powder, salt, and raisins.
◆ Beat together the egg, milk, and oil.
◆ Add the liquid to the dry ingredients all at once, and mix quickly together. Do not over-mix.
◆ Spoon the mixture into 12 greased 2½ inch deep muffin pans.
◆ Bake for about 20 minutes.
◆ Turn out onto a wire rack. Serve warm, split and buttered.

SWEET SUCCESS

If you need to use the same baking sheets to bake in batches, cool by running the back of the baking sheet under cold water and wiping the surface with a paper towel before regreasing.

Chocolate Caramel Pecan Bread

MAKES 9 ROLLS

2 cups all-purpose flour
½ oz fresh yeast
1 tsp sugar
½ cup tepid milk
½ tsp salt
2 tbsp butter
1 egg, beaten
2 tbsp butter, melted
2 oz semisweet chocolate
¼ cup pecan nuts, chopped
½ tsp mixed spice
⅓ cup granulated brown sugar

Glaze
4 oz semisweet chocolate
2 tbsp butter
1 tbsp honey

◆ Sift ½ cup of the flour into a bowl. Add the yeast, sugar, and milk and mix to a smooth batter. Leave in a warm place for 10-20 minutes or until frothy.

◆ Sift the remaining flour with the salt into a bowl and blend into the butter. Add to the yeast batter. Stir in the egg and mix to a soft dough.

◆ Knead on a lightly floured surface for about 5 minutes until smooth. Put into a lightly oiled bowl. Cover with plastic wrap and leave to rise in a warm place for about 1 hour or until double in size.

◆ Knock back the dough and knead well. Roll out to an oblong of about 12 x 19 inches. Melt together the butter and chocolate and brush over the dough.

◆ Mix together the nuts, spice and sugar and sprinkle over the dough.

◆ Roll up lengthways, like a jelly roll. Cut into 9 slices.

◆ Grease an 7 inch square cake pan. Place the slices, cut side down, in the pan. Cover with oiled plastic wrap and leave to rise in a warm place for about 30 minutes.

◆ Preheat the oven to 375˚F. Remove the plastic wrap and bake the bread in the oven for about 30 minutes.

◆ Turn out onto a wire rack. Melt together the chocolate, butter and honey. Drizzle over the bread while warm. Serve warm.

Danish Pastries

MAKES ABOUT 16

1 oz fresh yeast
¼ cup tepid water
4 cups all-purpose flour
a pinch of salt
¼ cup shortening
2 tbsp sugar
2 eggs, beaten
1¼ cups butter

Filling
¼ cup butter
¼ cup powdered sugar, sifted
3 oz semisweet chocolate, melted
¼ cup toasted almonds, finely chopped
a few drops of almond extract

Glaze
1 egg, beaten
honey

◆ Blend the yeast and water together.
◆ Sieve the flour and salt into a bowl and blend in the shortening. Stir in the sugar.
◆ Add the yeast liquid and eggs to the flour and mix to a smooth elastic dough. Knead lightly. Put into a lightly oiled bowl and cover with plastic wrap. Chill for 10 minutes.
◆ Soften the butter and shape into a flat oblong on waxed paper.
◆ Roll out the dough on a floured surface to a rectangle 3 times the size of the butter.
◆ Place the butter in the center of the dough and fold the dough over to enclose it. Press the rolling pin firmly along the open sides.
◆ Give the dough a quarter turn and roll out to a rectangle 3 times as long as it is wide.

◆ Fold into 3. Wrap in plastic wrap and chill for 10 minutes. Repeat the rolling and folding 3 more times.
◆ To make the filling, beat together the butter and powdered sugar. Beat in the chocolate, almonds and almond extract. Chill.
◆ Roll out the dough thinly and cut into 3 inch squares.
◆ Put a rounded teaspoonful of filling onto the center of each square. Bring 2 opposite corners of the dough to the center. Either seal with beaten egg or insert a wooden toothpick through.
◆ Place on a greased baking sheet. Cover with greased plastic wrap and leave to prove for about 30 minutes.
◆ Preheat the oven to 425°F. Brush the dough with beaten egg. Bake for about 20 minutes.
◆ Brush with a little honey while warm.

Chocolate Waffles

SERVES 4

¼ cups all-purpose flour
2 tbsp unsweetened cocoa powder
a pinch of salt
2 tsp baking powder
2 tbsp sugar
2 eggs, separated
1¼ cups milk
¼ cup butter, melted

To serve
4 tbsp Chocolate Syrup (see page 150)
4 tbsp maple syrup
¼-½ cup pecan nuts, chopped

◆ Sift together the flour, cocoa powder, salt, and baking powder. Stir in the sugar.
◆ Make a well in the center and add the egg yolks, milk, and butter. Stir well together.
◆ Whisk the egg whites until stiff. Fold lightly into the batter.
◆ Pour the batter into a heated waffle iron and cook.
◆ To serve, mix together the chocolate and maple syrup and stir in the nuts. Serve the waffles immediately with the sauce poured over.

 Hot Desserts

Banana Choc-Chip Pudding   91

Hot Chocolate Soufflé with White Chocolate
and Orange Sauce   92

Chocolate Fondue   92

Magic Chocolate Pudding   94

Baked Alaska   95

Apricot-Glazed White Chocolate Rice Pudding with
Bitter Chocolate Sauce   96

Cinnamon Chocolate Pain Perdu   98

Chocolate Upside-Down Pudding   99

Chocolate Crêpes with Pineapple and
Bitter Chocolate Sauce   100

Banana Choc-Chip Pudding

SERVES 4-5

½ cup butter or margarine
½ cup sugar
2 eggs, beaten
1¼ cups self-rising flour
2 tbsp unsweetened cocoa powder
approximately 2 tbsp milk
1 small banana, peeled and chopped
2 oz chocolate chips

Sauce
1 cup granulated brown sugar
2 tbsp butter
2 tbsp corn syrup
4 tbsp light cream

◆ Cream the butter or margarine and sugar together until light and fluffy.
◆ Gradually add the eggs, beating well between each addition.
◆ Sift together the flour and cocoa, and fold into the egg mixture. Add enough milk to give a soft dropping consistency.
◆ Stir in the banana and chocolate chips.
◆ Turn the mixture into a greased 4 cup bowl. Cover with greased waxed paper and foil with a central pleat in each. Secure with string. Steam for 1½ hours.

◆ To make the sauce, put all the ingredients into a saucepan and bring to the boil, stirring.
◆ Turn out the pudding and serve with warm sauce.

Hot Chocolate Soufflé with White Chocolate and Orange Sauce

SERVES 6

granulated sugar for sprinkling dish
4 oz semisweet chocolate, chopped
¼ cup unsalted butter, cut into pieces
4 eggs, separated
3 tbsp orange-flavor liqueur
¼ tsp cream of tartar
2 tbsp sugar
powdered sugar for dusting

Chocolate and orange sauce
3 oz good-quality white chocolate, chopped
6 tbsp whipping cream
2 tbsp orange-flavor liqueur
2 tbsp orange juice

◆ Preheat the oven to 475°F. Generously butter a 4½ cup soufflé dish. Refrigerate for 5 minutes to set the butter, then re-butter the dish. Lightly sprinkle the base and sides of the dish with sugar, then shake out any excess.

◆ Melt the chocolate and butter. Remove from the heat. Beat in the egg yolks and orange-flavor liqueur. Set aside to cool slightly, stirring occasionally.

◆ With an electric mixer, beat the egg whites and cream of tartar together until stiff peaks form. Sprinkle the sugar over and continue beating for 1 minute, until the sugar is incorporated and the whites are glossy.

◆ Fold the whites into the cooled chocolate mixture. Do not overwork the mixture. Pour into the prepared dish.

◆ Place on a baking sheet and bake for 5 minutes. Reduce the oven temperature to 425°F and bake for 10-12 minutes longer. The top of the soufflé should be set but the soufflé should jiggle when the baking sheet is moved; it should remain soft in the center.

◆ Meanwhile, prepare the sauce. Melt the chocolate with the cream, stirring frequently until smooth. Stir in the orange-flavor liqueur and orange juice. Strain into a sauceboat and set aside to keep warm.

◆ To serve, dust the top of the soufflé with powdered sugar. Transfer from the baking sheet to the prepared serving plate. Serve immediately; pass the sauce separately.

RIGHT *Hot Chocolate Soufflé with White Chocolate and Orange Sauce*

Chocolate Fondue

SERVES 4-6

8 oz semisweet chocolate
8 oz milk chocolate
1 cup light cream
3½ tbsp Kahlua (coffee liqueur)
or Tia Maria

◆ Break the chocolate into very small pieces and put into a heavy-based saucepan. Add the cream and melt slowly over a low heat, stirring constantly.

◆ Immediately before serving, stir in the liqueur.

◆ Small chunks of Madeira or other loaf cake, marshmallows, macaroons, whole strawberries, cherries, chunks of banana, pineapple, and apple all make tasty dippers.

Magic Chocolate Pudding

SERVES 4-5

1 cup self-rising flour, sifted
¼ cup sugar
3 tbsp unsweetened cocoa powder, sifted
a scant ½ cup walnuts, chopped
¼ cup butter, melted
½ cup milk
a few drops of vanilla extract

Sauce
¾ cup granulated brown sugar
3 tbsp unsweetened cocoa powder, sifted
a scant 1 cup + 4 tbsp boiling water

◆ Preheat the oven to 350°F. To make the sponge, put the dry ingredients into a bowl. Add the butter, milk and vanilla extract and mix to form a thick batter.
◆ Pour the mixture into a buttered 4 cup ovenproof bowl.
◆ To make the sauce, mix together the brown sugar, cocoa powder and boiling water. Pour this sauce over the batter.
◆ Bake in the oven for about 40 minutes. During cooking the chocolate sponge rises to the top, and a chocolate fudge sauce forms underneath.
◆ Serve with vanilla ice cream.

Baked Alaska

SERVES 6-8

4 cups chocolate ice cream
3 eggs
⅓ cup sugar
⅛ cup all-purpose flour
2 tbsp unsweetened cocoa powder
approximately ½ lb fruit (strawberries,
bananas, raspberries, or cherries)
¼ cup + 2 tsp Marsala or sweet sherry
4 egg whites
1 cup sugar

◆ Pack the ice cream into a 1 lb loaf pan lined with waxed paper. Freeze overnight.

◆ Preheat the oven to 400°F. Put the eggs and sugar into a bowl and whisk until thick and creamy, and the whisk leaves a trail.
◆ Sift the flour and cocoa and fold gently into the mixture.
◆ Turn into a greased and lined 9 inch pan. Bake in the oven for 12-15 minutes. Cool and remove the lining.
◆ Prepare the fruit by slicing it and removing pits if necessary. Put into a bowl with the Marsala or sherry.
◆ Whisk the egg whites until stiff. Whisk in the sugar a little at a time. Spoon the meringue into a piping bag fitted with a large star nozzle.

◆ Trim the edges of the sponge, then cut 1 inch strips from 2 sides of the cake to make an oblong slightly larger than the ice cream block.
◆ Preheat the oven to 450°F. Put the sponge on an ovenproof serving plate. Spoon the fruit and juices over the sponge.
◆ Remove the ice cream from the freezer and turn it onto the sponge. Remove the paper.
◆ Quickly pipe the meringue decoratively over the ice cream, covering it completely.
◆ Bake in the oven for 3-5 minutes until lightly browned. Cut into slices and serve immediately.

Apricot-Glazed White Chocolate Rice Pudding with Bitter Chocolate Sauce

SERVES 10

½ cup white raisins

3½ tbsp hot water

2 tbsp apricot brandy or orange-flavor liqueur

¼ cup medium- or long-grain white rice

1½ cups milk

1 cup water

⅛ cup butter

½ cup sugar

6 oz good-quality white chocolate, chopped

3 eggs

2 cups heavy cream

2 tsp vanilla extract

1 tsp ground cinnamon

½ tsp grated nutmeg

Apricot glaze

½ cup apricot jam

1 tbsp orange juice or water

1 tbsp apricot brandy or orange-flavor liqueur

Bitter chocolate sauce

¼ cup heavy cream

¼ cup apricot jam

6 oz bitter chocolate, chopped

2 tbsp apricot brandy or orange-flavor liqueur

◆ In a bowl, combine the white raisins, hot water, and apricot brandy. Leave to stand for at least 2 hours.

◆ In a heavy-based saucepan, combine the rice, 1 cup milk, water, butter, and ¼ cup sugar. Bring to the boil, stirring occasionally. Reduce the heat, cover and simmer for 18-20 minutes, just until liquid is absorbed.

◆ Meanwhile, preheat the oven to 300°F. Butter a 6-9 cup shallow baking pan or soufflé dish and set aside. In a saucepan over a low heat, melt the chocolate with the remaining milk, stirring frequently until smooth. Remove from the heat. In a large bowl, lightly beat the eggs, remaining sugar, cream, vanilla extract, cinnamon, and nutmeg. Slowly beat in the melted chocolate until well blended. Stir in the white raisins and any liquid. Stir the egg mixture into the cooked rice mixture until well blended, then pour into the baking pan. Cover with foil.

◆ Set the baking pan into a roasting pan. Fill the roasting pan with hot water to about halfway up the side of the baking pan. Bake for 30 minutes, uncover and bake for 15-20 minutes longer, until a knife inserted 2 inches from the edge of the pan comes out clean; the center should remain slightly moist. Run a sharp knife around the edge of the pan to loosen the pudding from the edge and prevent the center from splitting. Leave to cool for 1 hour.

◆ Meanwhile, prepare the glaze. In a saucepan over a medium heat, melt the apricot jam with the orange juice and apricot brandy or liqueur, stirring until smooth. Gently spoon over the top of the pudding to glaze.

◆ Prepare the chocolate sauce. In a saucepan over a low heat, bring the cream and apricot jam to a boil. Remove from the heat and stir in the chocolate, stirring until melted and smooth. Press through a sieve and stir in the apricot brandy or liqueur; keep warm. Serve with the glazed rice pudding.

SWEET SUCCESS

This pudding can be made in individual molds and unmolded for a more elegant presentation. Butter 10 ¾ cup custard cups or ramekins and line the base of each with waxed paper. Butter the paper. Bake for 3-5 minutes less than for the above recipe. Cool the puddings for at least 1 hour; do not glaze. Unmold each pudding onto a plate, remove the paper and top with a little warm glaze; spread evenly. Pour over a little chocolate sauce and serve the remainder separately.

Cinnamon Chocolate Pain Perdu

SERVES 4-6

⅓-½ cup butter
12-14 slices French bread
6 oz semisweet chocolate
2¼ cups milk
2 eggs
2 egg yolks
1 tsp ground cinnamon
¼ cup sugar
powdered sugar

◆ Preheat the oven to 375°F. Butter the slices of bread on both sides. Place on a baking sheet and bake in the oven for about 5 minutes or until lightly golden. Turn over and bake on the other side until golden, about 2-5 minutes.

◆ Melt the chocolate.

◆ Bring the milk almost to boiling point. Remove from the heat and whisk into the chocolate.

◆ Beat together the eggs, egg yolks, cinnamon, and sugar. Pour on the chocolate milk and whisk well.

◆ Arrange the French bread in a large shallow baking pan. Strain the chocolate custard over the bread.

◆ Put the dish into a roasting pan and pour in boiling water to come halfway up the side of the baking pan.

◆ Cook in the oven for 30-40 minutes until lightly set.

◆ Dredge with powdered sugar and serve with light cream.

Chocolate Upside-Down Pudding

SERVES 6

½ cup light brown sugar
¼ cup butter
4 pineapple rings
6 walnut halves
2 eggs, separated
2 tbsp butter, melted
⅔ cup granulated brown sugar
1 cup self-rising flour
2 tbsp unsweetened cocoa powder

◆ Preheat the oven to 350°F. Grease an 8 inch cake pan.

◆ Cream together the sugar and butter and spread over the base of the pan. Arrange the pineapple rings on the base, with a walnut in the center of each.

◆ Beat together the egg yolks and butter until creamy.

◆ Whisk the egg whites until stiff. Fold in the sugar and egg yolk mixture.

◆ Sift together the flour and cocoa and fold in carefully. Pour over the fruit and spread evenly.

◆ Bake in the oven for 30 minutes.

◆ Carefully turn out onto a serving dish and serve with pouring custard or light cream.

Chocolate Crêpes with Pineapple and Bitter Chocolate Sauce

MAKES 12

¼ cup all-purpose flour
1 tbsp cocoa powder
1 tsp sugar
¼ tsp salt
2 eggs
¾ cup milk
⅛ cup unsalted butter, melted plus
extra for reheating crêpes
1 tsp vanilla extract
vegetable oil for greasing

Pineapple filling
⅛ cup unsalted butter
1 pineapple, peeled, cored and cut into
½ inch pieces or 1 lb can pineapple
pieces in juice, drained
½ tsp ground cinnamon
¼ cup natural maple syrup
2 oz semisweet or milk chocolate chips
a scant ½ cup macadamia nuts,
chopped and toasted

Chocolate sauce
4 oz semisweet chocolate, chopped
6 tbsp water
3 tbsp natural maple syrup
⅛ cup unsalted butter, cut into pieces
powdered sugar for dusting
fresh cranberries or raspberries and
mint leaves for decoration

◆ Into a bowl, sift the flour, cocoa powder, sugar, and salt. Mix to blend; make a well in the center.

◆ In another bowl, lightly beat the eggs with the milk. Gradually add to the well in the center of the flour mixture. Using a whisk, blend in the flour from the sides of the bowl to form a paste, then a batter; beat until smooth. Stir in the melted butter and vanilla extract and strain into another bowl. Leave to stand for 1 hour.

◆ With a pastry brush, brush the bottom of a 7 or 8 inch crêpe pan with a little vegetable oil. Heat the pan over a medium heat. Stir the batter (if the batter is too thick, stir in a little milk or water; it should be thin). Fill a ¼ cup measure or small ladle three-quarters full with batter, then pour into the hot pan. Quickly tilt and rotate pan to cover the bottom of the pan with a thin layer of batter. Cook over a medium-high heat for 1-2 minutes, until the top is set and the bottom is golden. With a metal spatula, loosen the edge of the crêpe from the pan, turn over and cook for 30-45 seconds, just until set. Turn out onto a plate.

◆ Continue making crêpes, stirring the batter occasionally and brushing the pan lightly with oil. (A non-stick pan is ideal and does not need additional greasing.) Stack crêpes with sheets of waxed paper between each. Set aside.

◆ Prepare the filling. In a large skillet over medium-high heat, melt the butter until sizzling. Add the pineapple pieces and sauté until golden, 3-4 minutes. Sprinkle with cinnamon and stir in the maple syrup. Cook for 1-2 minutes longer, until the pineapple is lightly coated with syrup and the liquid has evaporated. Remove from the heat.

◆ Lay a crêpe on a plate or work surface, bottom side down. Spoon a little pineapple mixture onto the top half of the crêpe. Sprinkle over a few chocolate chips and macadamia nuts. Fold the bottom half over, then fold into quarters. Continue using all the crêpes, pineapple filling, chocolate chips and nuts. Set each one on a buttered baking sheet and cover tightly with foil until ready to serve.

◆ Prepare the chocolate sauce. In a medium saucepan over a low heat, melt the chocolate with water and maple syrup, stirring frequently until smooth and well blended. Stir in the butter. Keep warm.

◆ Preheat the oven to 375°F. Uncover the crêpes, brush the top of each with melted butter and re-cover tightly. Bake for 5 minutes just until heated through. Place on a dessert plate or individual plates. Dust with powdered sugar and decorate with fresh cranberries or raspberries and mint leaves. Serve the chocolate sauce separately.

COLD DESSERTS

Chocolate Mousse

SERVES 4-6

6 oz semisweet chocolate
2 tbsp honey
3 eggs, separated
½ oz powdered gelatin
3 tbsp hot water
¾ cup heavy cream

To serve
whipped cream
sliced bananas

◆ Put the chocolate and honey into a bowl over a pan of hot water and melt.
◆ Stir in the egg yolks and beat until smooth. Remove from the heat.
◆ Dissolve the gelatin in the water. Stir into the chocolate mixture. Chill until the mixture is the consistency of unbeaten egg white.
◆ Whip the cream until thick, but not stiff. Fold into the chocolate mixture.
◆ Whisk the egg whites until stiff and fold them into the chocolate mixture.

◆ Pour into a 4½ cup mold. Chill until set.
◆ Unmold onto a serving dish. Pipe whipped cream round the base and decorate with banana slices.

Fruited White Chocolate Bavarian Creams with Passion Fruit and Chocolate Sauces

SERVES 8

vegetable oil for molds
1½ cups whipping cream
4 oz good-quality white chocolate, chopped
2 tsp powdered gelatin
¼ cup + 2 tsp water
2 cups milk
4 egg yolks
¼ cup sugar
3 tbsp orange-flavor liqueur

Passion fruit sauce
6 very ripe passion fruit
¼ cup + 2 tsp orange juice
2 tbsp sugar or to taste
1 tsp cornstarch, dissolved in 1 tsp water
1 tbsp orange-flavor liqueur

Chocolate liqueur sauce
8 oz bitter chocolate, chopped
¼ cup unsalted butter, cut into pieces
¾ cup water
2-3 tbsp chocolate-flavor liqueur

To decorate
grated chocolate
fresh mint sprigs

◆ Lightly oil 8 heart-shaped or other molds. In a saucepan over low heat, bring ¾ cup cream to the boil. Add the white chocolate all at once, stirring until smooth. Set aside.

◆ Sprinkle the gelatin over the water in a bowl; leave to stand and soften.

◆ In a saucepan over a medium heat, bring the milk to the boil. In a bowl with a hand-held electric mixer, beat the egg yolks and sugar until thick and pale, 2-3 minutes. Reduce the mixer to the lowest speed, gradually beat in the milk, then return the custard mixture to the saucepan.

◆ Cook the custard over a medium heat, stirring constantly with a wooden spoon until the mixture thickens and coats the back of the spoon; do not boil or the custard will curdle. Remove from the heat and stir in the softened gelatin until dissolved, then stir into the chocolate mixture. Strain the custard into a large chilled bowl. Stir in the orange-flavor liqueur and refrigerate for about 20 minutes, until the mixture begins to thicken.

◆ In a bowl, with an electric mixer, beat the remaining cream until soft peaks form. Gently fold into the thickening gelatin-custard mixture. Spoon an equal amount into each mold. Place the molds on a baking sheet and refrigerate for 2 hours, or until set. Cover all the molds with plastic wrap and refrigerate for several hours.

◆ Prepare the passion fruit sauce. Halve the passion fruit crossways.

Scoop the juice and seeds into a saucepan. Stir in the orange juice, sugar and dissolved cornstarch. Bring to the boil, then simmer for 1-2 minutes, until the sauce thickens. Remove from the heat; cool slightly. Stir in the orange-flavor liqueur. Pour into a sauceboat.

◆ Prepare the chocolate sauce. In a saucepan over a medium heat, melt the chocolate and butter with water, stirring frequently until smooth. Remove from the heat and cool slightly. Stir in the chocolate-flavor liqueur and strain into a sauceboat.

◆ To serve, unmold the desserts onto plates at least 30 minutes before serving to soften slightly. Fill a bowl with hot water. Run a knife around the edge of each mold and dip into the hot water for 5-7 seconds. Dry the bottom of the mold; quickly cover the dessert with a plate. Invert the mold onto the plate giving a firm shake; carefully remove the mold.

◆ Spoon a little of each sauce around each heart-shaped Bavarian cream. Decorate with grated chocolate and fresh mint.

Chocolate Tiramisù

SERVES 14-16

Chocolate sponge fingers
¼ cup all-purpose flour
2 tbsp cocoa powder
2 tbsp instant coffee powder
¼ tsp salt
4 eggs, separated
½ cup fine granulated sugar
2 tsp vanilla extract
¼ tsp cream of tartar
powdered sugar for dusting

Chocolate mascarpone filling
17½ oz container mascarpone cheese,
at room temperature
¼ cup powdered sugar, sifted
1½ cups freshly brewed instant coffee
2¼ cups heavy cream
6 oz semisweet chocolate, melted and
cooled
6 tbsp coffee-flavor liqueur
2 oz semisweet chocolate, grated
2 tbsp chocolate-flavor liqueur

To serve
cocoa powder for dusting
whipped cream (optional)

SWEET SUCCESS

Mascarpone is an Italian cream cheese with a smooth creamy texture and soft, sweet flavor. It is available from supermarkets and specialty stores. A quicker version of this recipe can be made using about 7 oz bought sponge fingers. In either case, make this dessert at least 1 day ahead to allow the mixture to set firm and the flavors to mingle.

◆ Prepare the sponge fingers. Grease 2 large baking sheets and line with waxed paper. Grease and lightly flour the paper. In a bowl, sift together twice the flour, cocoa powder, coffee powder, and salt. Mix well and set aside.

◆ In another bowl, with an electric mixer, beat the egg yolks with ¼ cup sugar until thick and pale, 2-3 minutes. Beat in the vanilla extract.

◆ In a large bowl, with an electric mixer and cleaned beaters, beat the egg whites and cream of tartar until stiff peaks form. Sprinkle over the remaining sugar, 2 tbsp at a time, beating well after each addition.

◆ Fold 1 spoonful of egg whites into the egg-yolk mixture to lighten, then fold in remaining egg whites. Sift the flour mixture over and fold into the egg mixture, but do not overwork the mixture. Spoon the batter into a large piping bag fitted with a medium (about ½ inch) plain nozzle. Pipe the batter into about 30 5 inch or 24 4 inch sponge fingers. Dust with powdered sugar.

◆ Bake for 12-15 minutes, until set and tops feel firm when touched with a fingertip. Transfer to a wire rack to cool on baking sheets for 10 minutes. With a wide spatula, transfer the sponge fingers to wire racks to cool.

◆ With a hand-held electric mixer at low speed, beat the mascarpone cheese with the powdered sugar just until smooth. Gradually beat in ¼ cup coffee; do not overbeat.

◆ In another bowl, with an electric mixer, beat the cream until soft peaks form. Gently fold the cream into the mascarpone mixture. Divide the mixture in half. Fold the melted chocolate and 2 tbsp coffee-flavor liqueur into half until blended. Fold the grated chocolate and chocolate-flavor liqueur into the remaining mascarpone mixture. Set both mixtures aside.

◆ In a bowl wide enough to hold the sponge fingers, combine half the remaining instant coffee with 2 tbsp coffee-flavor liqueur. Quickly dip side of a sponge finger into the coffee mixture and place it dry-side down in a 13 x 9 inch cake pan; do not let the sponge fingers get too soggy or they may fall apart. Continue with about half the sponge fingers (you will need enough for 2 layers) to form a fairly close layer with not much space between each sponge finger. Drizzle over the remaining coffee mixture. Place the remaining coffee and coffee-flavor liqueur in the bowl.

◆ Pour the chocolate-mascarpone mixture over the bottom layer of sponge fingers, smoothing the chocolate mixture. Layer the remaining sponge fingers over the chocolate mixture, dipping them into the coffee mixture 1 at a time. Drizzle over any remaining coffee mixture. Pour the grated chocolate-mascarpone mixture over this layer and smooth the top, leaving no spaces between filling and sides of pan. Cover the pan tightly and refrigerate overnight. Dust the top with cocoa powder before serving. If you like, decorate with extra whipped cream.

White Chocolate Fruit Fools in Chocolate Cups

SERVES 12

12 chocolate cups (see page 18)

Mango purée
1 mango, peeled and cut into cubes,
with 4 cubes reserved for decoration
grated rind and juice of ½ orange
1 tsp lemon juice or to taste
1 tbsp sugar or to taste

Kiwi fruit purée
3 kiwi fruit, peeled and sliced, with 4
slices reserved for decoration
grated rind of 1 lime with
1-2 tsp juice
1 tbsp sugar or to taste

Cranberry-raspberry purée
½ cup fresh raspberries with berries
reserved for garnish
1 tbsp lemon juice
1 tsp sugar or to taste
8 oz can cranberry sauce

White chocolate mousse
4 oz good-quality white chocolate,
chopped
¼ cup milk
1 tbsp orange-flavor liqueur
1¼ cups heavy cream
2 egg whites
¼ tsp cream of tartar

◆ Prepare chocolate cups as directed on page 18, using 1½ lb semisweet chocolate and 1 tbsp white vegetable shortening and extra-large cupcake papers.
◆ Prepare the fruit purées in a food processor or blender, beginning with the lightest colour purée to avoid washing the processor after each purée. Place the mango cubes in the processor with the orange rind and juice. Process until smooth. Taste the purée and add lemon juice and sugar if necessary; this depends on the natural sweetness of the fruit. Scrape the purée into a bowl. Cover and refrigerate.
◆ Place the kiwi fruit slices into the processor with lime rind and juice. Process until smooth. Taste the purée and add more lime juice and sugar if necessary. Scrape the purée into a bowl. Cover and refrigerate.
◆ Place the raspberries, lemon juice and sugar into the food processor. Process until smooth. Press through a strainer into a bowl. Return to the food processor. Add the cranberry sauce and using the pulse action, process once or twice, just to blend, but leaving some texture to the purée. Taste the purée and add more lemon juice or sugar if necessary. Scrape the purée into small bowl. Cover and refrigerate.
◆ Prepare the mousse. In a saucepan over low heat, melt the white chocolate with the milk, stirring frequently until smooth. Remove from the heat and stir in the orange-flavor liqueur. Cool to room temperature.
◆ With a hand-held electric mixer, beat the cream until soft peaks form. Stir 1 spoonful of cream into the chocolate mixture to lighten, then fold in the remaining cream.
◆ In another bowl, with an electric mixer with clean beaters, beat egg

whites and cream of tartar until stiff peaks form. Fold into the chocolate-cream mixture. (You may not want to use all the egg whites if the mousse is soft enough; this depends on the brand of chocolate used.) Divide into 3 bowls.
◆ To assemble, arrange the prepared chocolate cups on 1 large or 2 smaller baking sheets (arrange adequate refrigerator space beforehand). Spoon a little of the mango purée into 4 chocolate cups. Spoon a little of the raspberry purée into 4 chocolate cups and then the kiwi fruit purée into the remaining 4 cups. Reserve a little of each purée for topping, then fold each of the purées into one of each of the 3 bowls of mousse; do not mix well – leave swirls of purée visible for effect. Spoon each fool mixture into the appropriate chocolate cups and top each with a decorative swirl of its matching purée. Refrigerate until ready to serve. Decorate each with a berry or a cube or slice of fruit. Refrigerate for at least 30 minutes or until firm.

SWEET SUCCESS

Pretty chocolate cups can be made using brioche molds or teacups. Line each mold or cup with a square of foil. Do not press tightly but allow it to form folds or soft pleats against the side of the mold or cup; be sure the bottom is flat. Spoon melted chocolate down the inside of the folds, using a zig-zag motion and turning the cup. This gives an uneven pleated look.

Chocolate Roulade

SERVES 6-8

6 oz semisweet chocolate
5 eggs, separated
¼ cup sugar
3 tbsp hot water
powdered sugar, sifted

Filling
scant 2 cups heavy cream
1 tbsp powdered sugar, sifted
2 tbsp unsweetened cocoa powder
2 tsp instant coffee
½ tsp vanilla extract

To decorate
powdered sugar
whipped cream
candied violets
angelica leaves

◆ Preheat the oven to 350°F. Melt the chocolate in a bowl over a pan of hot water.
◆ Put the egg yolks into a large bowl. Add the sugar and beat well until pale and fluffy.
◆ Add the hot water to the chocolate and stir until smooth. Whisk into the egg mixture.
◆ Whisk the egg whites until stiff. Lightly fold into the chocolate mixture. Pour into a greased and lined 15½ x 9½ inch jelly roll pan.
◆ Cook in the oven for 15-20 minutes, until firm.
◆ Remove from the oven. Cover with a sheet of waxed paper and a damp dish towel. Leave until completely cold.

◆ To make the filling put all the ingredients into a bowl. Whisk until thick. Chill.
◆ Turn the roulade onto a sheet of waxed paper dusted with powdered sugar. Peel away the lining paper.
◆ Spread the filling over the roulade to within 1 inch of the edge. Roll up like a jelly roll, using the waxed paper to help.
◆ Place seam-side down on a serving platter and chill for 1 hour before serving.
◆ To serve, dredge the roulade with powdered sugar. Pipe whipped cream down the center and decorate with candied violets and angelica leaves.

RIGHT *Chocolate Roulade*

Chocolate Cheesecake Cups

SERVES 6

1 lb cream cheese
3 eggs, separated
½ cup sugar
¼ cup sour cream
½ oz powdered gelatin
5 tbsp water
6 oz semisweet or milk chocolate, chopped
6 oz semisweet chocolate
6 individual pie dough cases (approx. 3 inches diameter)
chocolate caraque (see page 18), to decorate

◆ Put the cheese and egg yolks into a bowl. Add half of the sugar and beat well together.
◆ Stir in the sour cream.
◆ Dissolve the gelatin in the water.
◆ Whisk the egg whites until stiff. Whisk in the remaining sugar.
◆ Stir the gelatin into the cheese mixture.
◆ Fold the meringue and the chopped chocolate into the cheese mixture.
◆ Pour into 6 individual molds and chill until set.
◆ Melt the chocolate and spread over the underneath and outsides of the pastry cases. Place upside down over small glasses to set.

◆ Turn out the cheesecakes and place one in each chocolate cup.
◆ Serve decorated with chocolate caraque.

Triple Chocolate Mousse Parfaits

SERVES 6

Bitter chocolate mousse
4 oz bitter chocolate, chopped
¼ cup whipping cream
1 tbsp pieces unsalted butter
2 eggs, separated
1 tbsp rum
pinch of cream of tartar

Milk chocolate mousse
4 oz good-quality milk chocolate,
chopped
¼ cup whipping cream
2 tbsp pieces unsalted butter
2 eggs, separated
1 tbsp coffee-flavor liqueur
pinch of cream of tartar

White chocolate mousse
4 oz good-quality white chocolate,
chopped
¼ cup whipping cream
1 tbsp pieces unsalted butter
2 eggs, separated
1 tbsp chocolate-flavor liqueur
pinch of cream of tartar

To serve
7 tbsp chocolate sauce (see page 150)
¼ cup whipped cream
6 chocolate-coated coffee beans

◆ First prepare the bitter chocolate mousse. In a saucepan, melt the chocolate with cream, stirring frequently until smooth. Remove from the heat. Stir in the butter and beat in the egg yolks, 1 at a time, then stir in the rum. Allow to cool.
◆ With an electric mixer, beat the egg whites and cream of tartar until stiff peaks form; do not overbeat. Stir in 1 spoonful of egg whites into the chocolate mixture to lighten, then fold in the remaining egg whites.

◆ Using a ladle or tablespoon, carefully spoon an equal amount of mousse into each of 6 sundae, parfait or wine glasses. Do not touch the edge of the glasses; if any of the mixture drips, wipe the glass clean. Place the glasses on a tray or baking sheet and refrigerate for 1 hour, or until set.
◆ Prepare the milk chocolate mousse as above, then spoon equal amounts over the bitter chocolate mousse. Refrigerate for about 1 hour, or until set.
◆ Prepare the white chocolate mousse as above, then spoon equal amounts over the milk chocolate mousse. Cover each glass with plastic wrap and refrigerate for 4-6 hours or overnight, until set.
◆ To serve, spoon 1 tbsp chocolate sauce over each mousse. Spoon whipped cream into a small piping bag fitted with a medium star nozzle and pipe a rosette of cream on to each mousse. Decorate with chocolate-coated coffee beans.

Chocolate Pots de Crème

SERVES 8

2 cups milk
½ cup sugar
8 oz semisweet or bitter chocolate,
chopped
1 tbsp vanilla extract
3 tbsp brandy or liqueur
7 egg yolks

To decorate
whipped cream
chopped pistachios
chocolate leaves (see page 19)

◆ Preheat the oven to 325°F.
◆ In a saucepan, bring the milk and sugar to the boil. Add the chocolate all at once, stirring frequently until melted and smooth. Stir in the vanilla extract and brandy or liqueur.
◆ In a bowl, beat the egg yolks lightly. Slowly beat in the chocolate mixture until well blended. Strain the custard into a 9 cup measuring jug or large pitcher.
◆ Place 8 ½ cup *pots de crème* cups or ramekins into a shallow roasting pan. Pour an equal amount of custard into each cup. Pour enough hot water into the pan to come about halfway up the side of the cups.
◆ Bake for 30-35 minutes, until the custard is just set. Shake the pan slightly; the center of each custard should jiggle. Alternatively, insert a knife into the side of 1 custard; the knife should come out clean. Remove the pan from the oven and transfer the cups from the pan to a heatproof surface to cool completely.

◆ Place the cooled custards on a baking sheet and cover with plastic wrap. Refrigerate until well chilled. (The custards can be stored for 2 days in the refrigerator.)
◆ To serve, decorate the top of each custard with a dollop or rosette of whipped cream. Sprinkle each with chopped pistachios and a chocolate leaf.

Chocolate Trifle

SERVES 6

7 oz chocolate jelly roll
14 oz can apricot halves, drained
2¼ cups Chocolate Custard
(see page 151)
1¼ cups heavy cream, whipped

To decorate
chocolate hearts (see page 19)
miniature almond macaroons
maraschino cherries, etc

◆ Cut the jelly roll into ½ inch slices and arrange over the base and sides of a large serving bowl.
◆ Arrange the drained apricots on top.
◆ Pour the cold Chocolate Custard over the apricots.
◆ Pipe the whipped cream over the top. Decorate with chocolate hearts, the miniature almond macaroons, maraschino cherries etc, as desired.

RIGHT *Chocolate Trifle*

Chocolate-Glazed Chocolate Zuccotto

SERVES 8-10

1 chocolate roulade sponge
(see page 66)
½ cup Amaretto liqueur
1 lb ricotta or mascarpone cheese
½ cup sugar
2 cups whipping cream
1 tbsp vanilla extract
6 oz semisweet chocolate, melted
3 tbsp flaked almonds, toasted
and chopped
grated rind of 1 orange plus
3 tbsp juice
4 Amaretti cookies, broken into
small pieces
2 oz candied fruit, chopped

Chocolate sauce
¼ cup butter
2 tbsp corn syrup
4 oz semisweet chocolate, chopped
extra grated orange rind to decorate

◆ Prepare the chocolate roulade sponge as on page 66. Line a 12½ cup glass bowl with plastic wrap, allowing enough to fold over the bottom when the dessert is finished. Cut the cake in half lengthways. Cut each strip into triangle-shaped pieces. Sprinkle the cake pieces with 4 tbsp Amaretto liqueur and line the bowl with the cake pieces, leaving no open spaces and pressing the cake firmly against the sides of the bowl. Reserve the remaining cake pieces to make the bottom.
◆ If using ricotta cheese, press the cheese through a strainer into a large bowl. (This is not necessary for mascarpone cheese.) Beat the cheese and sugar until smooth.
◆ Beat the whipping cream with the vanilla extract until soft peaks form. Fold a spoonful of cream into the cheese mixture to lighten, then fold in the remaining cream. Divide the mixture in half. Into half, fold the melted chocolate and almonds; set aside. Into the other half, fold in the orange rind and juice, the remaining Amaretto liqueur, the Amaretti cookies and candied fruit.

◆ Spoon the cheese and Amaretti mixture into the cake-lined bowl to form an even layer all around the bowl. Spoon the chocolate mixture into the center and smooth the top. Cover the top with the remaining cake pieces and fold over the excess plastic wrap, pressing down lightly to create a flat bottom. Refrigerate for 6-8 hours or overnight, until very firm.
◆ Prepare the glaze. Melt the butter, corn syrup and chocolate, stirring frequently until smooth. Cool slightly until thickened but still pourable.
◆ Peel back the plastic wrap and unmold onto a serving plate; remove the plastic wrap. Pour the glaze over the top, using a metal spatula to spread it evenly and scrape excess off the plate. Clean the plate. Refrigerate for 5 minutes, until the chocolate is set. Cut strips of waxed paper into triangles and place over the dessert about 1½ inches apart. Dust with cocoa or powdered sugar. Decorate the top with orange rind. Refrigerate until ready to serve.

Frozen Chocolate and Cherry Mousse Ring

SERVES 8

8 oz semisweet chocolate, chopped
2 tbsp cherry-flavor liqueur
2 tbsp water
4 eggs, separated
¼ tsp cream of tartar
¼ cup sugar
¼ cup whipping cream

Poached cherries
2 lb fresh sweet cherries
1 orange
½ cup sugar
½ cup seedless raspberry jam or
redcurrant jelly
1 tbsp cornstarch, dissolved in
1 tbsp cold water

To serve
1 cup whipping cream
1 tbsp sugar
1 tbsp cherry-flavor liqueur
fresh mint leaves
chocolate-dipped cherries
(see page 137)

◆ Lightly oil a 5 cup freezerproof ring or other mold. Melt the chocolate with the cherry-flavor liqueur and water. Remove from the heat and beat in the egg yolks, 1 at a time, beating well after each addition.

◆ With an electric mixer, beat the egg whites and cream of tartar until soft peaks form. Gradually add the sugar, beating well, until the egg whites are stiff and glossy but not dry. Fold a spoonful of egg whites into the chocolate mixture to lighten, then fold in the remaining egg whites.

◆ With a hand-held electric mixer, beat the cream just until soft peaks form. Fold into the chocolate mixture, then pour the mousse into the prepared mold. Cover the mold with plastic wrap and freeze for 6-8 hours or overnight. (The mousse can be stored covered in the freezer for 1-2 days.)

◆ Prepare the cherries. Remove the stems and pits. Using a swivel-bladed vegetable peeler, remove the rind from the orange and squeeze the juice. Place in a saucepan with the sugar and water. Bring to the boil, then reduce the heat. Add the cherries to the poaching liquid and simmer for 7-10 minutes, until tender. Remove from the heat and leave the cherries in the poaching liquid for 3-4 hours.

◆ Using a slotted spoon, transfer the cherries from the liquid to a bowl. Add the raspberry jam and dissolved cornstarch to the syrup and bring to the boil, then reduce the heat and simmer for 1-2 minutes until the syrup is thickened and coats the back of a spoon. Strain over the cherries and cool to room temperature. Refrigerate until completely chilled.

◆ To unmold the mousse, run a thin-bladed knife around the outer and inner edges of mold. Dip the mold into warm water to come about halfway up the sides of the mold for 5 seconds. Dry the bottom of the mold; quickly cover the top with a large plate. Invert the mold onto the plate, giving a firm shake; remove the mold. Smooth the surface with a metal spatula and freeze for 5 minutes to chill the surface.

◆ To serve, beat the cream, sugar and cherry-flavor liqueur until soft peaks form. Spoon one-quarter of cream into a small piping bag fitted with a medium star nozzle and pipe a decorative border around the edge of the mold; spoon the remaining cream into the center of the mold. Decorate the outer edge with mint leaves and chocolate-dipped cherries and serve the cherries in their sauce separately.

Rich Chocolate Ice Cream

SERVES 4

8 oz semisweet chocolate, chopped
2 cups Half and Half or milk
3 egg yolks
¼ cup sugar
1½ cups heavy cream
1 tbsp vanilla extract

RIGHT *Rich Chocolate Ice Cream*

◆ In a saucepan over a low heat, melt the chocolate with ½ cup Half and Half or milk, stirring frequently until smooth. Remove from the heat.

◆ In a saucepan over a medium heat, bring the remaining Half and Half or milk to the boil. In a bowl, with a hand-held mixer, beat the egg yolks and sugar until thick and creamy, 2-3 minutes. Gradually pour the hot milk over the egg yolks, beating constantly, then return the mixture to the saucepan.

◆ Cook over medium heat until the custard thickens and lightly coats the back of a wooden spoon, stirring constantly; do not let the mixture boil or the custard will curdle. Immediately pour the melted chocolate over, stirring constantly until well blended.

◆ Pour the cold cream into a bowl and strain custard into the bowl with the cream. Blend well and cool to room temperature. Refrigerate until cold.

◆ Transfer the custard to an ice-cream maker and freeze according to the manufacturer's instructions. Leave to soften for 15-20 minutes before serving.

VARIATIONS

White, Dark or Milk Chocolate Chunk: *Stir 8 oz good-quality white, dark or milk chocolate, chopped, into the ice cream when removing from the ice-cream maker.*

Mocha Ice Cream: *Prepare the ice cream as directed but add 2 tbsp instant coffee powder, dissolved in 2 tbsp water, to the melted chocolate before adding to the custard.*

Chocolate Orange Pots

SERVES 8

6 oz semisweet chocolate
rind of 1 small orange, finely grated
3 eggs, separated
2-3 tbsp Curaçao
1 cup heavy cream

To decorate
whipped cream
orange rind spirals
chocolate orange sticks

◆ Put the chocolate into a bowl over a pan of hot water and melt.

◆ Remove from the heat and stir in the grated orange rind, egg yolks, and Curaçao. Stir well and leave to cool.

◆ Whip the cream until thick. Whisk the egg whites until stiff. Fold the cream and egg whites into the chocolate mixture.

◆ Pour into 8 individual pots (such as custard cups) and chill well.

◆ To serve, top with a spoonful of softly whipped cream and decorate with orange rind spirals and chocolate sticks.

Profiteroles

SERVES 6

¼ cup unsalted butter
¼ cup water
⅝ cup all-purpose flour
2 eggs, beaten

Filling
1¼ cups heavy cream
2 tbsp powdered sugar, sifted
a little Grand Marnier
2 tsp finely-grated orange rind

Chocolate sauce
4 oz semisweet chocolate
2 tbsp orange juice
⅛ cup powdered sugar
⅛ cup butter

◆ Melt the butter in a pan with the water.

◆ Bring to the boil and immediately tip in the flour. Beat well until the mixture forms a ball that comes cleanly away from the pan. Leave to cool.

◆ Preheat the oven to 400°F. Beat or whisk the eggs into the mixture, a little at a time. Continue beating until the mixture is smooth and glossy.

◆ Put the mixture into a piping bag fitted with a ½ inch plain nozzle. Pipe about 24 small balls onto a greased and floured baking sheet.

◆ Bake in the oven for 15-20 minutes until well risen and golden brown. A few minutes before removing from the oven, pierce them with a sharp knife to release the steam. Cool on a wire rack.

◆ To make the filling, whisk the cream until stiff. Stir in the powdered sugar, Grand Marnier, and orange rind. Put the cream in a piping bag fitted with a small nozzle and pipe the cream into the choux buns through the slits.

◆ To make the sauce, put all the ingredients into a bowl over a pan of hot water and heat until melted. Stir well together.

◆ Pile the profiteroles on a serving dish and just before serving, pour over the warm sauce.

Charlotte Louise

SERVES 8

18-20 sponge fingers
¼ cup unsalted butter
⅓ cup sugar
6 oz semisweet chocolate
1 cup ground almonds
1¼ cups heavy cream
½ tsp almond extract

To decorate
whipped cream
pistachio nuts
candied violets or roses
satin ribbon

◆ Cut a round of waxed paper to fit the base of a 6¼ cup Charlotte mold. Oil it lightly and place in the mold.
◆ Line the sides of the mold with the sponge fingers.
◆ Cream the butter and sugar together until light and fluffy.
◆ Melt the chocolate. Cool slightly, then beat into the butter together with the ground almonds.
◆ Whip the cream until thick, but not stiff. Add the almond extract. Fold into the chocolate mixture and mix well.
◆ Spoon the mixture into the lined mold. Press in firmly. Chill well.

◆ Turn out onto a plate. Remove the paper and pipe with whipped cream. Decorate with pistachio nuts and candied violets or roses. Tie a satin ribbon around the charlotte.

Chocolate Pavlova with Kiwi Fruit and Orange

SERVES 8-10

4 tbsp cocoa powder
1 tsp cornstarch
4 egg whites, at room temperature
¼ tsp salt
1 cup fine granulated sugar
1 tsp cider vinegar

White chocolate cream
4 oz good-quality white chocolate, chopped
½ cup milk
1 tbsp unsalted butter, cut into pieces
1 cup heavy cream
2 kiwi fruit, peeled and sliced
2 oranges, segmented

To decorate
fresh mint sprigs, wallflowers

◆ Preheat the oven to 325°F. Place a sheet of waxed paper on a large baking sheet and mark a 8 inch circle on it using a plate or cake pan as a guide. Into a bowl, sift together the cocoa powder and cornstarch; set aside.

◆ In another bowl, with an electric mixer, beat the egg whites until frothy. Add the salt and continue beating until stiff peaks form. Sprinkle in the sugar, 1 tbsp at a time, making sure each addition is well blended before adding the next, until stiff and glossy. Fold in the cocoa and cornstarch mixture, then fold in the vinegar.

◆ Spoon the mixture onto the circle on the paper, spreading the meringue evenly and building up the sides higher than the center. Bake in the center of the oven for 45-50 minutes, until set. Turn off the oven and leave the meringue to stand in the oven 45 minutes longer; the meringue may crack or sink.

◆ Meanwhile, prepare the chocolate cream. In a saucepan over low heat, melt the chocolate with the milk, stirring until smooth. Beat in the butter and cool completely.

◆ Remove the meringue from the oven. Using a metal spatula, transfer to a serving platter. Cut a circle around the center of the meringue about 2 inches from the edge; this allows the center to sink gently without pulling the edges in.

◆ When the chocolate mixture is completely cool, in a bowl, with an electric mixer, beat the cream until soft peaks form. Stir half the cream into the chocolate to lighten, then fold in the remaining cream. Spoon into center of the meringue.

◆ Arrange the kiwi fruit and orange in the center of the chocolate cream and decorate with fresh mint and wallflowers.

RIGHT *Chocolate Pavlova with Kiwi Fruit and Orange*

Pears and Chocolate Sauce

SERVES 6

4 oz semisweet chocolate
3 tbsp strong black coffee
3 tbsp apricot jam
a scant 4 tbsp water
4 tbsp heavy cream
large pinch of ground cinnamon
4-8 scoops vanilla or chocolate ice cream
6 ripe pears, peeled, halved and cored
crisp cookies (such as Langues de chat*), to serve*

◆ Put the chocolate, coffee, jam, and water into a small heavy pan. Slowly bring to the boil, stirring constantly.

◆ Remove from the heat and stir in the cream and cinnamon.

◆ Strain into a bowl and leave to cool.

◆ Put 1 or 2 scoops of ice cream in 6 individual serving dishes. Arrange 2 pear halves on each serving.

◆ Spoon over the chocolate sauce and serve immediately with crisp cookies.

Chocolate and Strawberry Frozen Daquoise

SERVES 10

1¼ cups sugar
2 tbsp cocoa powder, sifted
5 egg whites
¼ tsp cream of tartar
2½ cups good-quality chocolate
ice cream
2½ cups good-quality strawberry
ice cream
2 cups whipping cream
¼ cup sugar
2 tbsp raspberry-flavor liqueur

Strawberry sauce
1 lb frozen strawberries, drained
1 tbsp lemon juice

To decorate
12 oz fresh strawberries
10 chocolate-dipped strawberries
(see page 137)

◆ Preheat the oven to 275°F. Line 1 large and 1 small baking sheet with waxed paper or foil. Using an 8 inch cake pan or plate as a guide, mark 2 circles on the large baking sheet and 1 circle on the small baking sheet.

◆ In a bowl, mix together ¼ cup sugar and the cocoa powder. Set aside.

◆ With an electric mixer, beat the egg whites and cream of tartar until stiff peaks form. Gradually sprinkle the remaining sugar over, a little at a time, beating well after each addition, until the egg whites are stiff and glossy. Gently fold in the cocoa and sugar mixture just until blended.

◆ Spoon one-third of the meringue mixture inside each marked circle on the baking sheets. Spread each meringue out evenly to an 8 inch circle, smoothing the tops and edges.

◆ Bake the meringues for 1¼ hours, until crisp and dry. Transfer to wire racks to cool for 10 minutes on baking sheets. Then remove the meringues from the waxed paper or foil to cool completely; the meringues can be stored in an airtight container if they are not to be used at once.

◆ Place the meringue layers on a freezerproof serving platter and freeze for 20 minutes; this makes them firmer and easier to handle while spreading the ice cream. Meanwhile, remove the chocolate and strawberry ice creams from the freezer to soften for 15-20 minutes.

◆ Remove the meringue layers and serving platter from the freezer. Place 1 meringue layer on the platter and spread with chocolate ice cream to within ½ inch of the edge. Cover with a second meringue layer and spread with strawberry ice cream to within ½ inch of the edge. Top with the third meringue layer, pressing the layers gently together. Return to the freezer for 5–6 hours or overnight.

◆ In a bowl, with a hand-held mixer, beat the cream, sugar and raspberry-flavor liqueur until soft peaks form. Remove the meringue layers from the freezer and spread the top and sides with cream in a swirling or decorative pattern. Freeze until ready to serve if not using at once.

◆ For the sauce, process the strawberries in a food processor with a metal blade attached, until well blended. Press the purée through a sieve into a bowl. Stir in the lemon juice and if the sauce is too thick, thin with a little water.

◆ To serve, slice fresh strawberries lengthways and decorate the top of the daquoise. Serve each slice with some strawberry sauce and a chocolate-dipped strawberry.

Snowball Pie

SERVES 6

8 oz semisweet chocolate
¼ cup butter
a scant 1 cup crisp rice cereal
1¼ cups vanilla ice cream
1¼ cups chocolate ice cream
1¼ cups strawberry ice cream

To serve
Chocolate or Fudge Sauce
(see pages 150–151)
long shreds of coconut, toasted

◆ Melt the chocolate and butter together.
◆ Stir in the crisp rice cereal and mix well together.
◆ Press the mixture over the base and up the sides of an 8 inch pie plate. Place in the freezer until firm.
◆ Arrange alternate scoops of the ice cream.
◆ Pour over the sauce and sprinkle with the coconut. Serve immediately.

Chocolate Frozen Yogurt

SERVES 4-6

5 cups plain low-fat yogurt
1¼ cups + 2 tbsp sugar
6 tbsp cocoa powder
1 tbsp skim milk powder, dissolved in
1-2 tbsp milk or water

◆ In a bowl, with a wire whisk, mix together the yogurt, sugar, cocoa, and dissolved skim milk powder until smooth and well blended and the sugar is dissolved. Refrigerate for 1 hour, until cold.

◆ Transfer the yogurt mixture to an ice-cream maker and freeze according to the manufacturer's instructions; this mixture will not freeze as hard as ice cream. Transfer to a freezerproof serving bowl or container and freeze for 3-4 hours, until firm. (Frozen yogurt can be stored in the freezer for 2-3 weeks in a freezerproof container.)

VARIATION

For mocha frozen yogurt, use coffee-flavor low-fat yogurt and add 1 tbsp instant coffee powder, or experiment with other flavors.

Fruit-Studded Chocolate Marquise with Whiskey Custard Cream

SERVES 12-14

¼ cup white raisins
¼ cup chopped, stoned prunes
scant ¼ cup chopped, dried apricots
6 tbsp Scotch or apricot brandy
12 oz semisweet chocolate, chopped
1 cup unsalted butter, cut into pieces
4 eggs, separated
¼ tsp cream of tartar

Whiskey custard cream
2 cups Half and Half
2 large eggs
½ cup sugar
2 tbsp Scotch or apricot brandy

RIGHT *Fruit-Studded Chocolate Marquise with Whiskey Custard Cream*

◆ In a bowl, mix all the dried fruit with the Scotch or brandy. Leave to stand for at least 2 hours, stirring occasionally.
◆ Line a 9 x 5 inch loaf pan with plastic wrap, allowing enough to fold over the bottom when the marquise is finished.
◆ In a saucepan over low heat, melt the chocolate and butter, stirring frequently until smooth. In a bowl, with a hand-held electric mixer, beat the egg yolks until pale and thick, 3-4 minutes. Stir into the warm chocolate mixture and cook over low heat for 1 minute, stirring constantly until the mixture thickens and looks shiny. Remove from the heat and cool, stirring occasionally. Stir in the fruit and any remaining Scotch or brandy.
◆ With an electric mixer, beat the egg whites and cream of tartar until stiff peaks form; do not overbeat. Stir 1 large spoonful of egg whites into the chocolate mixture to lighten, then fold in the remaining egg whites.

◆ Spoon into the pan. Chill just until firm, then fold over the excess plastic wrap to cover the marquise. Refrigerate for at least 6 hours or overnight.
◆ Prepare the custard cream. In a saucepan over medium heat, bring the Half and Half to the boil. Remove from the heat. In a bowl, beat the eggs and sugar until well blended, about 1 minute.
◆ Pour the hot cream over and return the mixture to the saucepan over a low heat. Cook for 4-5 minutes, stirring constantly with a wooden spoon until the mixture thickens and just coats the back of the spoon; do not boil or the sauce will curdle. Strain into a chilled bowl and stir in the Scotch or brandy. Refrigerate until ready to use.
◆ To serve, slide the marquise and its base onto a rectangular serving dish. Refrigerate until ready to serve. Cut into thin slices and serve with whiskey custard cream.

Chocolate Hazelnut Bombe

SERVES 6-8

2¼ cups vanilla ice cream
a scant ½ cup hazelnuts or filberts, finely chopped and toasted
2¼ cups Chocolate Ice Cream (see page 116)
2 tbsp dark rum

To decorate
1¼ cups heavy cream, whipped
whole hazelnuts or filberts

◆ Put a 5 cup bombe mold or pudding basin into the freezer overnight.
◆ Soften the vanilla ice cream and mix in the hazelnuts or filberts. Line the bombe mold with the ice cream and freeze.
◆ Soften the chocolate ice cream and blend in the rum. Fill the center of the bombe. Cover with waxed paper and freeze.
◆ To serve, turn out the bombe onto a plate. Pipe with whipped cream and decorate with whole hazelnuts or filberts. Serve cut into wedges.

Easy Frozen Chocolate-Mint Soufflé

SERVES 6

9 oz semisweet chocolate, broken into pieces
2 cups heavy cream
4 eggs, separated
3-4 tbsp mint-flavor liqueur or
1 tbsp peppermint extract
¼ tsp cream of tartar
¼ cup sugar
grated chocolate for decoration

Chocolate-dipped mint leaves
20-24 fresh mint leaves
4 oz semisweet chocolate, chopped

◆ Prepare the chocolate-dipped leaves. Rinse the mint leaves in cold water and pat dry with paper towels. Line a baking sheet with waxed paper.
◆ In the top of a double boiler over a low heat, melt the chocolate, stirring frequently until smooth. Leave to cool to just below body temperature.

RIGHT *Easy Frozen Chocolate-Mint Soufflé*

Holding the stem end, dip each mint leaf about halfway into the chocolate, coating both sides, leaving excess chocolate to drip into the bowl. Place the coated leaves on a baking sheet and refrigerate; these leaves can be prepared 1-2 days ahead and kept refrigerated.
◆ Prepare a collar for the soufflé dish. Cut a piece of waxed paper or foil long enough to encircle the dish, allowing a 2 inch overlap. Fold the paper or foil in half lengthways and wrap around the dish so the collar extends about 3 inches above the sides of the dish. Secure the paper or foil with tape or kitchen string. Lightly oil the paper collar; set the dish aside.
◆ Place the chocolate in a food processor fitted with the metal blade or in a blender.
◆ In a saucepan, bring the cream to the boil. With the food processor or blender running, slowly pour the cream over the chocolate. Continue processing or blending until smooth, scraping the side of the container once.

◆ With the machine still running, add the egg yolks, 1 at a time, processing well after each addition until well blended; the chocolate mixture will be thick and creamy. Scrape into a bowl and stir in the liqueur. Cool to room temperature; the chocolate mixture will thicken further.
◆ With an electric mixer, beat the egg whites and cream of tartar just until stiff peaks form. Add the sugar, 2 tbsp at a time, and continue beating just until the egg whites are stiff and glossy; do not overbeat.
◆ Stir 1 large spoonful of egg whites into the chocolate mixture to lighten, then gently fold in remaining egg whites. Pour into the dish and freeze overnight. (The soufflé can be prepared 2-3 days ahead.)
◆ To serve, remove the tape or string from the sides of the dish and, using a knife as a guide, carefully unwrap the paper or foil from the dish and soufflé. Press the grated chocolate onto the side of the soufflé and top with a few chocolate-coated mint leaves. Serve the remaining leaves with each portion of soufflé.

Choc-Chestnut Mont Blanc

SERVES 6-8

¼ cup unsalted butter
2 tbsp sugar
6 oz semisweet chocolate, melted
12 oz chestnut purée
1-2 tbsp sherry

To decorate
whipped cream
miniature almond macaroons
candied chestnuts
grated chocolate

◆ Cream the butter and sugar together until light and fluffy.
◆ Beat in the melted chocolate.
◆ Blend in the chestnut purée and sherry.
◆ Pile the mixture into the center of individual dessert dishes and form into mountain shapes. Chill.
◆ Spoon or pipe a capping of whipped cream on the summit. Decorate the base with the miniature almond macaroons and candied chestnuts. Sprinkle with grated chocolate if you wish.

CANDIES

Chocolate-Dipped Caramel Apples

MAKES 12

vegetable oil
12 small apples, well scrubbed
and dried
⅛ cup pecans, walnuts, or filberts,
finely chopped and toasted (optional)
6 oz chocolate, chopped

Caramel Coating
2¼ cups heavy cream
1½ cups corn syrup
3 tbsp unsalted butter, cut into pieces
1 cup granulated sugar
a scant ⅔ cup brown sugar
pinch of salt
1 tbsp vanilla extract

◆ Oil a baking sheet with the vegetable oil. Insert a wooden lollipop stick firmly into the stem end of each apple; do not use metal sticks or small pointed wooden skewers as they could be harmful to children.

◆ Prepare the caramel coating. In a heavy-based saucepan, stir the cream, syrup, butter, sugars, and salt. Cook over medium heat, stirring occasionally, until the sugars dissolve and the butter is melted, about 3 minutes. Bring the mixture to the boil and cook, stirring frequently, until the caramel mixture reaches 240°F (soft ball stage) on a sugar thermometer, about 20 minutes. Place the bottom of the saucepan in a pan of cold water to stop cooking or transfer to a small, cold saucepan. Cool to about 220°F; this will take 10-15 minutes. Stir in the vanilla extract.

◆ Holding each apple by the wooden stick, quickly dip each apple into the hot caramel, turning to coat on all sides and covering the apple completely. Scrape the bottom of the apple against the edge of the saucepan to remove the excess; place on the prepared baking sheet. If necessary, reheat the caramel slightly to thin it. Leave the apples to cool for 15-20 minutes, until the caramel hardens.

◆ If using, place the nuts in a bowl. In the top of a double boiler over a low heat, melt the chocolate, stirring frequently until smooth. Remove from the heat. Dip each caramel-coated apple about two-thirds of the way into the chocolate, allowing the excess to drip off, then dip into the nuts. Place on a waxed paper-lined baking sheet. Leave to set for 1 hour, until the chocolate hardens.

Meringue Mushrooms

MAKES ABOUT 8

1 egg white
¼ cup fine granulated sugar
2 oz semisweet chocolate, melted
cocoa powder, to serve

◆ Preheat the oven to 275°F. Whisk the egg white until stiff.
◆ Whisk in the sugar a little at a time until the mixture is stiff and glossy.
◆ Put the meringue into a piping bag fitted with a ½ inch plain nozzle.
◆ Line a baking sheet with waxed paper. Pipe 6-8 small mounds of meringue about 1 inch in diameter to form the mushroom caps.
◆ Next pipe 6-8 smaller mounds, drawing each one up to a point, to represent the stalks.

◆ Bake in the oven for about 1 hour until dry and crisp. Allow to cool.
◆ Using the point of a sharp knife, make a tiny hole in the base of each mushroom cap.
◆ Spread a little melted chocolate on the underside of each cap and gently push on a stalk. Allow to set.
◆ Before serving, dust the mushrooms with a little cocoa powder.

Chocolate Fudge

MAKES ABOUT 1½ LB

2 cups sugar
¾ cup milk
½ cup butter
6 oz semisweet chocolate
¼ cup + 1 tbsp honey

◆ Put all the ingredients into a heavy-based saucepan.
◆ Stir continuously over a gentle heat until the sugar is completely dissolved.
◆ Bring to the boil and cook to the soft ball stage, 240°F.
◆ Remove from the heat and dip the base of the pan in cold water to stop further cooking.

◆ Leave for 5 minutes. Then beat the mixture with a wooden spoon until thick and creamy and beginning to "grain". Before it becomes too stiff, pour into a buttered 8 inch square pan. Leave to set.
◆ Using a greased knife, cut into 1 inch squares. To store the fudge, put in a tin between layers of waxed paper.

Chocolate Caramel Popcorn

SERVES 3-4

¼ cup brown sugar
⅛ cup butter
1½ tbsp corn syrup
1 tbsp milk
2 oz chocolate chips
a pinch of bicarbonate of soda
5 cups popped popcorn

◆ Preheat the oven to 300°F. Put the sugar, butter, syrup, and milk into a heavy-based saucepan.

◆ Stir over a gentle heat until the butter and sugar have melted. Bring to the boil.

◆ Boil without stirring for 2 minutes.

◆ Remove from the heat. Add the chocolate and bicarbonate of soda. Stir until the chocolate is melted.

◆ Measure the popped popcorn into a bowl. Pour over the syrup and toss well until evenly coated.

◆ Spread the mixture on a large baking sheet. Bake in the oven for about 15 minutes. Test for crispness. Bake for a further 5-10 minutes if necessary. Cool.

Chocolate Turtles

MAKES ABOUT 30

vegetable oil
Caramel Coating (see page 133)
a scant 2 cups filberts, pecans,
walnuts, or unsalted peanuts
or a combination
12 oz semisweet chocolate, chopped
3 tbsp white vegetable shortening

◆ Oil 2 baking sheets with the vegetable oil. Prepare the caramel coating.

◆ When the caramel has cooled for a few minutes, stir in the nuts until they are coated. Do not overwork or the caramel will become grainy. Using an oiled tablespoon, drop spoonfuls of caramel-nut mixture onto the prepared baking sheet, about 1 inch apart. If the caramel-nut mixture becomes too hard, reheat over low heat for several minutes until softened. Refrigerate until firm and cold.

◆ Using a metal spatula, transfer the nut clusters to a wire rack over a baking sheet to catch the drips. In a saucepan over a low heat, melt the chocolate and vegetable shortening, stirring occasionally until smooth; cool the chocolate to about 88°F.

◆ Using a tablespoon, spoon the chocolate over the nut clusters, being sure to coat completely, spreading the chocolate over the surface. Return the drips to the saucepan and reheat gently to completely cover all the clusters. Leave to set for about 2 hours at room temperature. Store in a cool place in an airtight container with foil between the layers, but do not refrigerate.

Chocolate-Dipped Fruit

MAKES ABOUT 12

*about 12 pieces of fruit, such as
strawberries; cherries; orange
segments; kiwi fruit; fresh peeled
lichees; Cape gooseberries; pitted
prunes; pitted dates; dried apricots;
dried pears; nuts*
*6 oz good-quality white chocolate,
chopped*
3 oz semisweet chocolate, chopped

◆ Clean and prepare the fruit. Wipe the strawberries with a soft cloth or brush gently with a pastry brush; wash and dry firm-skinned fruits such as cherries and grapes. Dry well and set on paper towels to absorb any remaining moisture. Peel or cut any other fruits being used. Dried or candied fruits can also be used.

◆ In the top of a double boiler over a low heat, melt the white chocolate, stirring frequently until smooth. Remove from heat and cool to tepid, about 84°F, stirring frequently.

◆ Line a baking sheet with waxed paper or foil. Holding the fruit by the stem or end and at an angle, dip about two-thirds of the fruit into the chocolate. Allow the excess to drip off and place on the baking sheet. Continue dipping the fruit; if the chocolate becomes too thick, set over hot water again briefly to soften slightly. Refrigerate the fruit until the chocolate sets, about 20 minutes.

◆ In the top of the cleaned double boiler over low heat, melt the semisweet chocolate, stirring frequently until smooth. Remove from the heat and cool to just below body temperature, about 88°F.

◆ Remove each white chocolate-coated fruit from the baking sheet and holding each by the stem or end, and at the opposite angle, dip the bottom third of each piece into the dark chocolate, creating a chevron effect. Set on the baking sheet. Refrigerate for 5 minutes, or until set. Remove from the refrigerator 10-15 minutes before serving to soften the chocolate.

Chocolate-Coated Toffee

1 cup pecans (optional)
1 cup unsalted butter,
cut into pieces
1½ cups sugar
¼ tsp cream of tartar
6 oz semisweet chocolate,
finely chopped

◆ Preheat the oven to 350°F. Place the pecans (if using) on a small baking sheet and bake for 10-12 minutes, until well toasted. Leave to cool completely, then chop and set aside.

◆ Line a 9 inch square cake pan with foil. Invert the pan and mold the foil over the bottom. Turn the tin right side up and line with the molded foil. Generously butter the bottom and sides of the foil.

◆ In a heavy-based saucepan over a medium heat, melt the butter. Stir in the sugar and cream of tartar, stirring until the sugar dissolves. Bring the mixture to the boil. Cover the pan for 2 minutes so steam washes down any sugar crystals which collect on the side of the pan. Uncover and continue cooking for 10-12 minutes, or until the toffee reaches 310°F on a sugar thermometer.

◆ Carefully pour into the pan and leave to rest for about 1 minute. Sprinkle the top of the toffee with chocolate and leave for 2 minutes until the chocolate softens. Using the back of a spoon or a wide-bladed knife, spread the chocolate evenly over the toffee until smooth. Sprinkle evenly with the chopped pecans (if using). Cool to room temperature, then refrigerate until firm and cold.

◆ Using the foil as a guide, remove the toffee from the tin. With the back of a heavy knife or hammer, break the toffee into large, irregular pieces. Store in an airtight container for about a week in the refrigerator.

RIGHT *Chocolate-Coated Toffee*

Chocolate Eggs

4 medium eggs
8 oz semisweet or milk chocolate
3 oz praline, ground finely
3 tbsp cream

◆ Using an egg prick or pin, pierce a hole at the pointed end of each egg.

◆ Using small scissors, carefully enlarge the hole to about ½ inch.

◆ Push a toothpick into the hole to puncture the yolk. Shake the raw egg into a bowl.

◆ Run water gently into the shells and shake until they are clean. Turn upside down and leave to dry.

◆ Melt the chocolate. Stir in the praline and cream. Spoon or pour the chocolate into the dry shells. Leave until set.

◆ Seal the holes with small round labels and place the eggs in an egg box, holed side down.

Chocolate-Mint Crisps

MAKES ABOUT 30

vegetable oil for greasing
4 tbsp sugar
¼ cup + 2 tsp water
1 tsp peppermint extract
8 oz semisweet chocolate, chopped

◆ Grease a baking sheet with vegetable oil. Set aside. In a saucepan, bring the sugar and water to the boil, swirling the pan until the sugar dissolves. Boil rapidly until the sugar reaches 280°F on a sugar thermometer. Remove the pan from the heat and stir in the peppermint extract. Pour onto the greased baking sheet and allow to set; do not touch as the sugar syrup is very hot and can cause serious burns.

◆ When the mixture is cold, use a rolling pin to break it up into pieces. Place the pieces into a food processor fitted with the metal blade and process until fine crumbs form; do not overprocess.

◆ Line 2 baking sheets with waxed paper or foil; grease the paper or foil. In the top of a double boiler over a low heat, melt the chocolate, stirring frequently until smooth. Remove from the heat and stir in the ground mint mixture.

◆ Using a teaspoon, drop small mounds of mixture onto the prepared baking sheets. Using the back of the spoon, spread into 1 inch circles. Cool, then refrigerate to set, at least 1 hour. Peel off the paper or foil and store in airtight containers with waxed paper between each layer. Store in the refrigerator for 1 week.

Chocolate-Stuffed Figs and Prunes

MAKES 24

12 large fresh figs
12 extra-large pitted prunes,
preferably presoaked or softened
3 tbsp unsalted butter, softened
½ cup blanched almonds, chopped
and toasted
1 egg yolk
1 tbsp Amaretto liqueur
3 oz semisweet chocolate, melted
and cooled

Chocolate for dipping
8 oz semisweet chocolate, chopped
5 tbsp unsalted butter, cut into pieces

◆ In a food processor fitted with the metal blade, process the butter, almonds, egg yolk, and liqueur until creamy. With the machine running, slowly pour in the melted chocolate and process until well blended. Scrape into a bowl and refrigerate for about 1 hour, until firm enough to pipe.

◆ Line a baking sheet with waxed paper. Pipe the mixture into the figs and prunes. Place the filled fruits on the baking sheet and chill for 30 minutes.

◆ In a saucepan over a low heat, melt the chocolate and butter, stirring frequently until melted and smooth. Leave to cool to room temperature, about 30 minutes, stirring occasionally.

◆ Insert a toothpick into each filled fruit. Dip each into the melted chocolate and allow the excess to drip off. Using another toothpick, push the fruit off the inserted toothpick onto the lined baking sheet. Alternatively, dip the filled fruits about two-thirds of the way into the chocolate, leaving one-third exposed. Place on the baking sheet. Refrigerate for at least 1 hour to set.

◆ Using a thin-bladed knife, remove the fruit from the baking sheet to cupcake papers. Remove from the refrigerator about 30 minutes before serving.

White Chocolate Fudge Layer

MAKES 36 TRIANGLES

1¼ lb good-quality white chocolate, chopped
14 oz can sweetened condensed milk
2 tsp vanilla extract
1½ tsp white vinegar or lemon juice
pinch of salt
2 cups unsalted macadamia nuts
6 oz semisweet chocolate, chopped
3 tbsp unsalted butter, cut into pieces
1 oz semisweet chocolate, melted, for piping

◆ Line an 8 inch square cake pan with foil. Invert the pan. Mold the foil over the bottom, then turn the cake pan right side up and line with the foil. Grease the bottom and sides of the foil. Set aside.

◆ In a saucepan over a low heat, melt the chocolate with the condensed milk, stirring frequently until smooth. Remove from the heat and stir in the vanilla extract, vinegar, and salt until well blended. Stir in the nuts. Spread half of the white chocolate mixture in the pan. Refrigerate for 15 minutes or until firm; keep the remaining mixture warm.

◆ In a saucepan over a low heat, melt the chopped chocolate and butter, stirring frequently until smooth. Cool slightly; pour over the white chocolate layer and refrigerate until firm, about 15 minutes.

◆ If necessary, gently reheat the remaining white chocolate mixture then pour over the set chocolate layer, smoothing the top evenly. Refrigerate for 2-4 hours, until completely firm.

◆ Using the foil as a guide, remove the set fudge from the pan. With a knife, cut into 16 squares. Cut each square diagonally in half, making 36 triangles. Place the fudge triangles onto a wire rack placed over a baking sheet to catch the drips.

◆ Spoon the melted chocolate into a small paper cone and drizzle chocolate over the fudge triangles. Store in an airtight container in the refrigerator for 1-2 weeks.

RIGHT *White Chocolate Fudge Layer*

Rocky Road Fudge

MAKES ABOUT 1½ LB

1 lb milk chocolate
¼ cup butter
2 tbsp light cream
1 tsp vanilla extract
a scant ½ cup walnuts, chopped
4 oz marshmallows, cut into small pieces with wetted scissors
1½ cups powdered sugar, sifted
3 oz semisweet chocolate, to decorate

◆ Melt the chocolate and butter in a bowl over a pan of hot water. Stir in the cream and vanilla extract.

◆ Remove from the heat and stir in the walnuts, marshmallows, and powdered sugar.

◆ Spread in an 8 inch square pan, lined with waxed paper.

◆ Chill until firm.

◆ Melt the semisweet chocolate. Using a piping bag fitted with a plain nozzle, drizzle the chocolate over the fudge. Leave to set.

◆ To serve, cut the fudge into diamond shapes.

Easy Chocolate Truffles

MAKES ABOUT 45

¼ cup whipping cream
9 oz semisweet chocolate, chopped
2 tbsp brandy or other liqueur
(optional)
4 tbsp cocoa powder

◆ In a saucepan over a low heat, bring the cream to the boil. Remove the pan from the heat. Add the chocolate all at once, stirring frequently until smooth. Stir in the liqueur if using. Strain into a bowl and cool to room temperature. Refrigerate for 1 hour, until thickened and firm.

◆ Line 2 small baking sheets with foil. Using a melon baller, a 1 inch ice-cream scoop, or a teaspoon, form the mixture into 1 inch balls and place on the baking sheets. Refrigerate for 1-2 hours, until the balls are firm.

◆ Place the cocoa powder in a small bowl. Drop each chocolate ball into the cocoa and turn with your fingers to coat with cocoa. Roll the balls between the palms of your hands, dusting with more cocoa if necessary. Do not try to make them perfectly round; they should look slightly irregular. Place on the baking sheets. Add more cocoa to the bowl if necessary.

◆ Shake the cocoa-coated truffles in a dry sieve to remove excess cocoa, then store, covered, in the refrigerator for up to 2 weeks or freeze for up to 2 months. Soften for 10 minutes at room temperature before serving.

Chocolate-Coated Raspberry Truffles

MAKES ABOUT 24

22 oz bitter chocolate, chopped
⅓ cup unsalted butter, cut into pieces
½ cup seedless raspberry jam
2 tbsp raspberry-flavor liqueur
12 oz chocolate, chopped

◆ In a saucepan over low heat, melt 10 oz chocolate, butter, and jam, stirring frequently until smooth and well blended. Remove from the heat and stir in the liqueur. Strain into a bowl and cool. Refrigerate for 2-3 hours, until firm.

◆ Line a baking sheet with waxed paper or foil. Using a melon baller, a 1 inch ice-cream scoop, or a teaspoon, form the mixture into balls. Place on the baking sheet and freeze for 1 hour, or until very firm.

◆ In the top of a double boiler over low heat, melt the remaining chocolate, stirring frequently until smooth; the chocolate should be 115°-120°F. Remove from the heat and pour into a clean bowl; cool to about 88°F.

◆ Using a fork, dip the truffles, 1 at a time, into the chocolate, coating completely and tapping the fork on the edge of the bowl to shake off the excess. Place on the prepared baking sheet. Refrigerate until the chocolate is set, about 1 hour. Store in an airtight container with paper towels covering the truffles to collect any moisture for up to 2 weeks or 1 month in freezer.

Milk Chocolate and Pistachio-Coated Truffles

MAKES ABOUT 24

½ cup heavy or whipping cream
12 oz good-quality milk chocolate,
chopped
1 tbsp unsalted butter
1 tbsp almond-flavor liqueur
12 oz bitter chocolate, chopped
a scant 1 cup shelled and unsalted
pistachio nuts, finely chopped

◆ In a medium saucepan over a medium heat, bring the cream to the boil. Remove from the heat. Add the chocolate all at once, stirring until melted. Stir in the butter and liqueur. Strain into a bowl. Refrigerate for 1 hour or until firm.
◆ Line a baking sheet with waxed paper or foil. Using a melon baller, a 1 inch ice-cream scoop, or a teaspoon, form the mixture into balls. Place on a baking sheet and freeze for 1 hour, or until very firm.
◆ In the top of a double boiler over a low heat, melt the bitter chocolate, stirring frequently until smooth; the chocolate should be about 115°-120°F. Remove from the heat and pour into a clean bowl; cool to about 88°F.

◆ Place the pistachios in a bowl. Using a fork, dip the truffles, 1 at a time, into the chocolate, coating completely and tapping the fork on the edge of the bowl to shake off the excess. Immediately drop into the bowl of pistachios and roll to coat the chocolate completely. Place on the prepared baking sheet. Refrigerate until set, about 1 hour. Store in an airtight container with paper towels covering the truffles to collect any moisture for up to 2 weeks or 1 month in the freezer.

RIGHT *Milk Chocolate and Pistachio-Coated Truffles*

Rich Chocolate Truffles

MAKES ABOUT 30

8 oz semisweet or milk chocolate
½ cup butter, diced
2 tsp liqueur (eg Tia Maria,
Cointreau, rum or brandy)
a scant 1 cup powdered sugar
ground nuts

◆ Melt the chocolate. Remove from the heat.
◆ Add the butter and liqueur and beat until smooth.
◆ Beat in the powdered sugar.
◆ Chill well until firm.
◆ Shape into 1 inch balls and roll in the nuts.
◆ To serve, place in cupcake papers and keep cool.

$\mathcal{S}$AUCES

Tobler Sauce

SERVES 4

8 oz Toblerone chocolate
¼ cup heavy cream

◆ Cut the chocolate into very small pieces. Put into a small pan and melt very quickly.

◆ Stir in the cream. Mix until smooth and immediately pour over ice cream or fruit such as bananas or pears.

SWEET SUCCESS

If you need to use the same baking sheets to bake in batches, cool by running the back of the baking sheet under cold water and wiping the surface with a paper towel before regreasing.

Chocolate Sauce

SERVES 3-4

4 tbsp cocoa powder
5 tbsp corn syrup
¼ cup butter
¼ cup milk
½ tsp vanilla extract

◆ Put the cocoa, corn syrup, and butter into a small pan. Heat gently until well blended.
◆ Stir in the milk and vanilla extract.
◆ Bring to the boil and simmer gently for about 3 minutes. Serve hot or cold.

VARIATIONS

Chocolate/Orange Sauce: Omit the vanilla extract. Add the grated rind of ½ orange.

Chocolate Syrup

SERVES 3-4

2 cups granulated brown sugar
¼ cup cocoa powder
1¼ cups boiling water
2 tsp vanilla extract

◆ Mix together the sugar and cocoa powder.
◆ Add the water, stirring continuously.
◆ Put the mixture into a small pan and simmer gently for 5 minutes, stirring frequently.
◆ Cool. Add the vanilla extract.
◆ Cover and chill in the refrigerator.

FUDGE SAUCE

CHOCOLATE SAUCE

CHOCOLATE SYRUP

Fudge Sauce

SERVES 4-6

1 tbsp cocoa powder
6 oz can evaporated milk
3 oz semisweet chocolate, grated
⅛ cup butter
2 tbsp granulated brown sugar

◆ Put the cocoa and evaporated milk into a pan and whisk well together.
◆ Add all the remaining ingredients. Heat gently, stirring, until the chocolate, sugar and butter have melted. Do not boil. Serve hot or warm.

Chocolate Custard

MAKES 2½ CUPS

2½ cups milk
6 egg yolks
¼ cup sugar
4 oz semisweet chocolate, grated

◆ Put the milk into a saucepan and bring almost to the boil. Remove from the heat.
◆ Whisk the egg yolks and sugar together until thick and fluffy.
◆ Gradually pour the milk onto the eggs and sugar, whisking continuously.
◆ Return the mixture to the saucepan and stir over a very gentle heat, until it coats the back of a spoon.

◆ Remove from the heat and add the chocolate. Stir until dissolved.
◆ Serve the custard hot or cold. To cool the custard, pour into a bowl and place dampened waxed paper directly onto the surface to stop a skin from forming. Chill.

Mars Bar Sauce

SERVES 4

4 Mars Bars
6½ tbsp heavy cream

◆ Dice the Mars Bars. Put in a small pan and melt very gently.
◆ Stir in the cream. Mix until smooth and immediately pour over ice cream.

DRINKS

Deluxe Chocolate Egg Nog

SERVES 10-12

9 oz semisweet chocolate, chopped
2 cups milk
6 eggs
¼ cup sugar
½ cup brandy or rum
½ cup Amaretto liqueur
2 tbsp vanilla extract
2 cups whipping cream
grated chocolate or cocoa powder
to decorate

◆ In a saucepan over a low heat, melt the chocolate and 1 cup milk, stirring frequently until smooth. Remove from the heat and stir in the remaining cold milk until well blended. Cool to room temperature.

◆ With an electric mixer, beat the eggs and sugar until pale and thick, 5-7 minutes. Gradually beat in the cooled chocolate, brandy, liqueur, and vanilla extract.

◆ In another bowl, with a hand-held electric mixer, beat the whipping cream just until soft peaks form. Stir a spoonful of cream into the chocolate-egg mixture then fold in the remaining cream. Chill.

VARIATION

To prepare without alcohol, omit the brandy and liqueur and substitute 1 cup milk, chocolate milk or cream.

Continental Hot Chocolate

MAKES 1 CUP

1½ oz semisweet chocolate, chopped
1½ tsp cocoa powder
pinch of salt
½ tsp sugar
milk

◆ Place the chocolate, cocoa powder, salt, and sugar in a small saucepan. Take the cup in which the chocolate will be served, fill it about one-quarter full of milk and then add enough water to almost fill the cup.

◆ Add the milk and water to the saucepan and, over medium heat, bring to a boil, beating constantly until the chocolate is melted and smooth. Boil for 30 seconds longer, beating until foamy, then pour into the cup. Serve immediately.

Spicy Hot Cocoa

SERVES 4

⅓ cup sugar
3 tbsp cocoa powder
½ tsp grated nutmeg
½ tsp ground cloves
½ tsp ground ginger
½ cup cold water
3 inch cinnamon stick, broken
into pieces
1 tsp vanilla extract
4 cups milk
marshmallows or whipped cream
to decorate

◆ In a saucepan, combine the sugar, cocoa powder, nutmeg, cloves, and ginger. Gradually stir in the water until the mixture is smooth. Add the cinnamon pieces and bring to the boil, stirring constantly. Cook for 1 minute longer, stirring constantly.
◆ Gradually beat in the milk and bring the mixture to below the boil (do not boil), beating constantly until the mixture is frothy. Remove from the heat, beat in the vanilla extract and strain into large cups or mugs. Top each with a few marshmallows or a dollop of whipped cream.

VARIATION

Minty Hot Chocolate: Prepare as above but omit the nutmeg, cloves, ginger, cinnamon, and vanilla. After the milk is beaten in, beat in 2 tbsp mint-flavor liqueur or 1 tbsp peppermint extract.

Velvety Hot Chocolate

SERVES 2

4 oz semisweet chocolate, chopped
3 tbsp cold water
2 tbsp hot water
2 cups milk
whipped cream to decorate

◆ In the top of a double boiler over a low heat, melt the chocolate and cold water, stirring frequently until smooth. Remove from the heat and beat in the hot water, beating until smooth. Pour into a small pitcher or 2 large cups or mugs.
◆ In a saucepan, bring the milk to the boil and pour into a separate pitcher, or pour some of the milk into each cup or mug of chocolate. Top with whipped cream. Serve at once.

Rich Iced Chocolate

SERVES 2

1 cup whipping cream
4 oz semisweet chocolate, chopped
2 tsp vanilla extract
2 cups freshly brewed espresso coffee, chilled
sugar to taste
grated chocolate to decorate (optional)

◆ In a small saucepan over a medium heat, bring the cream to the boil. Add the chocolate all at once, stirring until smooth. Remove from the heat and stir in the vanilla extract. Strain into a bowl. Cool to room temperature. Refrigerate for about 1 hour to chill but do not allow the chocolate to set.

◆ To serve, beat the cold espresso coffee into the chilled chocolate until well blended and frothy. Fill 2 tall glasses one-quarter full with crushed ice, then pour the chocolate-coffee mixture over. Sprinkle with grated chocolate.

Extra-Chocolate Milk Shake

SERVES 2

4 tbsp cocoa powder
½ cup sugar
½ cup water
6 tbsp corn syrup
1 tsp vanilla extract
½ cup cold milk
1 tbsp chocolate-flavor liqueur
1¼ cups chocolate ice cream
chocolate curls or grated chocolate to decorate

◆ First make the chocolate syrup. In a saucepan over a medium heat, combine the cocoa and sugar. Gradually stir in the water until smooth and well blended. Stir in the corn syrup, then bring to the boil, stirring frequently.

◆ Cook for 2-3 minutes, stirring constantly, until the mixture is smooth and thickened. Remove from the heat and stir in the vanilla extract. Cool slightly.

◆ In a blender or milk-shake machine, combine the milk, chocolate syrup, and liqueur (if using). Blend for 30 seconds. Add the ice cream and blend for about 45 seconds, just until smooth. Pour into 2 tall glasses and decorate with chocolate curls or grated chocolate.

Chocolate Cream Liqueur

MAKES ABOUT 5 CUPS

1 tbsp instant coffee powder
2 tbsp cocoa powder
1 cup milk
1 cup heavy cream
14 oz can condensed milk
1 egg yolk
1 cup Scotch
6 tbsp light rum
1 tbsp vanilla extract
1 tbsp coconut extract

◆ In a large, heavy-based saucepan, combine the coffee and cocoa powders. Gradually stir in the milk until the powders are dissolved. Stir in the cream and condensed milk and bring to the boil.

◆ In a bowl, lightly beat the egg yolk. Pour about 1 cup hot cream mixture over the egg yolk, beating well, then stir the cream-and-egg mixture back into the pan. Cook for 2-3 minutes longer until the mixture thickens and coats the back of a spoon. Remove from the heat. Stir in the Scotch, rum, and vanilla and coconut extracts. Strain into a bowl and cool to room temperature, stirring occasionally. Refrigerate for 2-3 hours until well chilled.

◆ Transfer to a bottle or jar with a tight-fitting lid and store in the refrigerator. Shake before serving.

FROM TOP RIGHT, CLOCKWISE: *Continental Hot Chocolate, Spicy Hot Cocoa and Velvety Hot Chocolate*

Iced Caribbean Chocolate

SERVES 4

1¼ cups milk
¼ cup light cream
2 large pinches of ground nutmeg
2 large pinches of ground cinnamon
1 large pinch of ground allspice
6 tbsp Chocolate Syrup (see page 150)

To serve
ice cubes
coffee ice cream

◆ Put the milk, cream, spices, and syrup into a bowl and whisk well together. Chill well.
◆ Before serving, whisk again.
◆ To serve, pour into glasses over ice cubes and top with scoops of coffee ice cream.

Choconana Milk Shake

SERVES 2-3

1¼ cups milk
4 tbsp Chocolate Syrup (see page 150)
2¼ cups chocolate ice cream
1 banana, cut into pieces
bought chocolate flake bars to serve

◆ Put the milk, chocolate syrup, ice cream, and banana into a blender.
◆ Cover and blend until smooth.
◆ To serve, pour into glasses and add a chocolate flake to each one.

ᘒNDEX